# 100 BIRDS

*and How They Got Their Names*

ALSO BY DIANA WELLS

*100 Flowers and How They Got Their Names*

# 100 BIRDS

*and How They Got Their Names*

DIANA WELLS

*Illustrated by*

*Lauren Jarrett*

ALGONQUIN BOOKS OF CHAPEL HILL

2002

Published by

ALGONQUIN BOOKS OF CHAPEL HILL

POST OFFICE BOX 2225

CHAPEL HILL, NORTH CAROLINA 27515-2225

a division of
Workman Publishing
708 Broadway
New York, New York 10003

Library of Congress Cataloging-in-Publication Data
Wells, Diana, 1940–
    100 birds and how they got their names / by Diana Wells ;
    illustrated by Lauren Jarrett.
        p. cm.
    Includes bibliographical references.
    ISBN 1-56512-281-X
    1. Birds—Nomenclature (Popular).    I. Title: One
hundred birds and how they got their names.    II. Title.
    QL677 .W45 2001
    598'.01'4—dc21                                    2001041390

10   9   8   7   6   5   4   3   2

For C. A. W.,

brilliant example of mate selection,

and all our children

# CONTENTS

........................................................................................................

# Contents

# Contents

# ACKNOWLEDGMENTS

I needed, and received, a great deal of help with this book. Especially appreciated were the professional skills and unflagging enthusiasm of Peter Kupersmith, Janet Klaessig, Charlie Colombo and the rest of the staff at the Joseph Krauskopf Memorial Library, Delaware Valley College, Pennsylvania. I thank my brother, David Greig (loved all my life, but lover of birds long before me) for his help. Also David Steward for his contagious fondness for birds. Eric Salzman gave me valuable ornithological advice, and my copy editor Bonnie Thompson rescued me from many a blunder. Henrietta Leyser raids the Bodleian library on demand, Claire Wilson keeps me alert with her uncompromising grammatical integrity, Inea Bushnaq guides me in Arabic language and culture, and Leslie Hartnett took time to read the manuscript. My brother, Andrew Greig, advised me on Australia. I thank Amy Gash for her affectionate encouragement and firm but tender editing. I thank Elisabeth Scharlatt and all the Algonquin staff for their trust, and Betsy Amster for being my excellent agent. I thank Peg Stevens for making it seem possible (when it didn't). And I thank John and Bar Purser and Geraldine Lloyd for the walk on which they showed me the dipper.

# INTRODUCTION

I n the most inhospitable places on earth we find birds: sailors tossing on the lonely, stormy seas see ocean birds following their ships; antarctic explorers were met by upright, curiously formal penguins, clustering round to see who had arrived on their bleak ice floes; in the middle of the most arid deserts sand grouse nest, flying miles to soak their feathers with water to bring back for their thirsty young; high above the tree line on craggy mountains there are birds; in the long darkness of sleepless nights we hear owls hunting.

It is hard to imagine a place in the world without birds. Indeed a world without birds would be hell itself. In the Sixth Book of *The Aeneid* Virgil wrote, "The descent into Hell is easy" ("Facilis descensus Averno"). The word for hell, "Averno," means "a place without birds," from the Greek *a* "without," and *ornis,* "bird." Avernus, the entrance to hell, was a toxic Italian lake, the fumes from which were said to kill all birds.

"All birds are called Birds," claims a medieval bestiary, "but there are a lot of them . . . there are so many sorts . . . that it is not possible to learn every one." How true for most of us this still is. Even with binoculars, books and cameras, the names of birds still elude us. Not only is it hard to distinguish one bird from another, but the names themselves are confusing. Speaking for myself, I found that birds were not like flowers, whose names had become familiar to me with my first book, and anyway seemed easier to learn. Flowers stay put to be identified, but birds fly away far too quickly. The flash in the bushes too often disappeared long before I could get my glasses adjusted, and sometimes when I had a bird and its name nicely sorted I then found it had been reclassified and I had to start again! Real birders (or twitchers as they are called in Britain) love this challenge, and make lists of birds they have seen and identified, the rarer the better. They travel for miles, squat in muddy bogs, tear their clothes in briars and rise at unwelcoming hours, when the rest of us are sybaritically turning over in bed, or lazily making toast and watching what we glibly call "sparrows," "thrushes," and "robins" at our bird feeders.

"A robin *is* a robin, is a robin," we faintly gasp when confronted with a World Checklist of scientific bird names, or a knowledgeable birder in a bog. But we do need to know a little more, if only because robins in America and in Britain are entirely different birds. Blackbirds, orioles, sparrows, warblers, to name only some, refer to different birds in different places.

In America, many birds were named by early naturalists, often European, who sometimes called them after similar birds back home. Mark Catesby, an English naturalist who explored the southern states in the early eighteenth century, wrote that "Very few of the Birds having Names consigned to them . . . except some which had Indian Names, I have call'd them after European birds." Catesby would have caused less confusion and fewer ornithological headaches if he had taken notice of the names used by the "Indians." Some of the headaches have been shared by me as I have tried to unravel these confusions.

It's a pity if confusion with names puts us off and lessens our enjoyment of some of the loveliest creatures on earth. People can, and always have, enjoyed birds without knowing much about them. On the other hand, to name something can be to understand it a little better. "To know one thing from another," wrote Linnaeus, "permanent distinct names must be given . . . recorded and remembered." In 1753 he began sorting the names of plants, animals and birds, and we have been using his system ever since. But Linnaeus would not have wanted us to tremble at the thought of names, for he was trying to simplify, not complicate the system. Latin was the common language of his time, used by scientists to write to one another. Linnaeus himself refused to learn any contemporary European language but his native Swedish, and he couldn't have envisaged a time when all naturalists didn't speak Latin.

All scientific names are Latinized, even if their origins are Greek or from the names of places or people. Linnaeus's new system gave each creature, and plant, two names, that of its genus (or kind), and that of its species (or individual characteristic). Before that, scientific names were long and descriptive. Even if we find our present system hard, using only two (or sometimes three) names, was a great improvement. Linnaeus grouped genera into families, and families into orders. An order (or group of families) always has a name ending in the suffix "-iformes," and a family name always ends with the suffix "-idae."

The name of the genus is a noun (capitalized), followed by the name of the species, an adjective (not capitalized). Birds are also grouped into subfamilies, tribes and qualifying specific names, but I have tried to avoid these and keep scientific names as simple as possible.

We aren't helped by taxonomists *changing* names, because a bird can be reclassified and renamed if it is found to belong to a different group than previously thought. In our era of DNA testing, this happens rather often. It is of small comfort to know that otherwise the accepted name is the one given by Linnaeus in January 1758, or the first name recorded after that date, even if this name seems inappropriate or was misspelled.

Understanding bird names is a combination of ornithology, taxonomy, and etymology, all professional fields, and none of them my own. Nor can I hope to touch on more than a few birds in one short book. But looking at names, at how birds were called in the past and why, connects us to our close relationship with them. Birds have been part of our lives since the beginning of human time. Some of the earliest Egyptian and Persian gods were in the form of birds. Greek gods were shaped like humans, but sometimes even they turned into birds to lure or punish mortals with whom they were so reassuringly intimate.

Part of this fascination with birds was the ability (of most of them) to fly, toward where we thought heaven might be. If, like Icarus, we fell, it was not because of inadequate wings, but because of our inadequate attachment of them. Our angels (unless they are "fallen angels"), still have the feathery wings of birds, not the wings of bats or beetles. It doesn't seem to bother us that the wings attached to their shoulders couldn't possibly get them airborne. For angels lack the powerful muscles attached to a deep-keeled breastbone, which birds developed in order to fly, and angels don't, as far as I know, have the light, toothless jaws or hollow bones of birds. If they have human voice boxes, our angels could never sing like birds either. Birds make their music in a voice box (or syrinx) placed much lower than ours, where the bronchial tubes divide. Unlike humans, birds can vary their song by taking in air from two directions rather than one. Perhaps that's why our angels are often equipped with harps and lutes.

Not all birds fly or sing sweetly either, but a bird is differentiated from other creatures because it has feathers. Feathers are evolutionary miracles, and nothing we can invent equals them. They are strong and stiff enough to resist air pressure (and be used by us as pens), warm enough to keep penguins cozy in the antarctic (and soft enough to pillow the heads of human potentates).

Birds have been used (and abused) by us as far back as we know. They were eaten, they were kept in cages for their songs, their feathers were used for warmth and decoration. Their ways were used to guide us too. The Greeks knew that when swallows arrived, spring was near. The Vikings loosed birds from their ships and followed the direction in which they flew to find new lands. The Romans used birds to help them make decisions, by dividing the sky into quarters and watching how birds flew across. This practice was called augury, and gave us the word "auspice," from the Latin *aves specere,* "to watch birds."

Nowadays we are apt to rely more on computer projections to predict our future, but these results are sometimes dismissed as "for the birds."

Birds are in our language, whether we know it or not. In the old days, horse droppings on the streets were only good "for the birds" (usually sparrows) to eat. When we "hoodwink" someone we are using a term to describe sealing the eyes of a hunting bird to keep it docile. When we do something with "panache" we are being jaunty, as if wearing a feather (Latin *pinnaculum*) on our hat. When we are "ravenous" we will, like a raven, eat anything.

It was always true that I loved words and birds. But the study of birds is the sole occupation of many people, and I never could hope to have their expertise. To write about birds was, for me, bold indeed. My greatest encouragement came from a letter written by Alexander Wilson to the famous naturalist William Bartram. Wilson came to America from Scotland at the end of the nineteenth century. He was a weaver, a poet and a political reformist. Soon after his arrival he decided he was a "wretch separate from the great chain of nature," and he began to study American birds, even though he knew nothing about them. Wilson sent Bartram a descriptive list of birds, asking him to "Be pleased to mark the Names of each with a pencil as except 3 or 4 I dont know any of them." From these three or four names, Wilson eventually went on to write the first, and one of the most comprehensive books on American birds ever. It is not now an ultimate authority, but it is still useful today, and wonderfully readable. Wilson went out into the field himself to observe and collect his own information. Naturalists like him were called "field" as opposed to "closet" (or "cabinet") naturalists, who were sent specimens to classify but didn't venture into the wild. Ornithologists today expect to go out and study birds for themselves.

I confess to being a "closet naturalist." I do not struggle through thorny mires at dawn to spot an unknown bird, and if you were to ask me to identify a bird I might pretend to have lost my spectacles. Lists still frighten me, and I confuse Latin names. But for all my ignorance, birds are in my blood now, in a way they never could have been before I began this book, and I look at them anew.

I always knew what a curlew looked like, but had never seen one. Last year I saw a curlew in Scotland, and I felt my world had changed forever. I wanted nothing more than that curlews should be on the moors forever. Like all passions, my love is now tinged with a fear of loss. When I knew birds less, I didn't worry much about whether they had enough space to live in the world along with us. The more I came to know them, the more I valued these wondrous creatures. Emily Dickinson wrote about these only feathered beings that we know:

"Hope" is the thing with feathers—
That perches in the soul—
And sings the tune without the words—
And never stops—at all—

Without hope, without feathers, we would be—lost in hell.

# 100 BIRDS

*and How They Got Their Names*

# ALBATROSS

Albatrosses fly as if by magic, rarely flapping their long, narrow wings. At different heights above the ocean wind speeds vary dramatically. Albatrosses glide down swiftly to meet low-speed surface winds, which then thrust them up again, and they repeat this to soar almost indefinitely. To sailors long ago this seemed supernatural, and they thought the birds were incarnations of wandering souls. To kill an albatross, they believed, would bring bad luck to the ship and its crew.

"An albatross around one's neck" has been part of our language ever since Samuel Taylor Coleridge wrote of the cursed seaman in "The Rime of the Ancient Mariner"; but in spite of his vivid description of the great bird circling the ship and perching on the rigging like "a Christian soul," it is unlikely that Coleridge saw a living albatross. The story probably originated in 1759 from Captain George Shelvocke's account in his *Voyages,* which described an albatross soaring around the ship, following "as if he had lost himself" and making "our display with sail, reef and rudder" seem "clumsy and inept." His ship, the *Speedwell,* was battling to round Cape Horn in terrible weather, and one sailor had already been lost overboard in the icy sea. The second in command was Simon Hatley, who in a fit of "melancholy," shot the albatross in September 1719, and was blamed for the ship's continued bad luck. Hatley had been imprisoned by the Spaniards and punished for privateering by being "hanged until [he was] almost strangled and then cut down." This torture is reminiscent of the heavy albatross around the Ancient Mariner's neck.

**♫ Albatrosses fly as if by magic; sailors thought the birds were incarnations of wandering souls.**

Although sailors were in awe of these birds, they did sometimes kill and eat them, and even made purses out of their webbed feet. The albatross's common name has prosaic roots. It originates from the Arabic *al-qudus,* "bucket," describing seabirds that hold water in their bills (*see* Pelican). This became *alcatraz* in Spanish (which now means "gannet"). The Latin *alba* means "white," and mature albatrosses of some species are largely white, which may explain the change to "albatross."

Albatrosses are in the order Procellariiformes, from the Latin *procella,* meaning a violent storm. These ocean birds live in turbulent southern oceans remote from land. Their bills are "tubed" to excrete excess salt from the seawater they drink (*see* Petrel). They can't fly when they are becalmed. Although they come ashore to breed, a pair often won't even wait for their chick to fledge; the parents will feed it enough so that it can survive alone on its fat until making its way to the sea.

The albatross family, the Diomedeidae, is called after Diomedes, the king of Aetolia, who fought in the Trojan War. On his way home he stopped on an Adriatic island; there his companions were punished for grumbling by being turned into birds, "like white swans, though they were not swans," wrote Ovid. Despite the wandering albatross's obvious difference from swans, Linnaeus named the legendary bird after Diomedes's men, calling it *Diomedea exulans,* or "homeless." This bird has a wingspan of up to twelve feet and travels hundreds of miles. It is now thought to return to favorite fishing areas rather than wandering aimlessly.

The only albatross that regularly visits North American waters is the black-footed albatross, *D. nigripes,* but few of us will see even this bird. Still, the albatross is with us, a powerful symbol of sin and retribution. We wonder, too, like Coleridge's Wedding Guest, what our duties to the natural world should be.

# AVOCET

In June 1814, John James Audubon rose at dawn to watch nesting avocets on a lake in Indiana. "Now Reader," he writes, "wait a few moments until I eat my humble breakfast . . . [and] you and I will do our best to approach the sitting bird unseen by it." He does this successfully: "Lovely bird," he murmurs, "how innocent, how unsuspecting, and yet how near to thine enemy, albeit he be an admirer of thy race!" At this point the Reader might prefer to be excused, leaving Audubon to shoot five avocets, including three incubating females. Perhaps we should remind ourselves that in those days, before photography and good binoculars, shooting a bird was the only way to examine it properly, and avocets, like other birds, once seemed too plentiful ever to become rare.

The American avocet that Audubon described is mostly white, with a chestnut head during mating season, and black markings on the wings. White birds often have black wing tips, because black feathers are stronger than pigmentless white ones and wear better on the edges of wings. The American avocet has long blue legs and an upward-curving bill, which accounts for the family name Recurvirostridae, from the Latin *recurvo,* "I bend back-ward," and *rostrum,* "beak." The members of this family include the stilts. The American avocet and the black-necked stilt breed in North America. Stilts have thin red legs, even longer than the avocets'. The stilt's name, *Himantopus,* is from the Greek *himantos,* "thong," and *pous,* "foot."

The avocet's common name comes from the old European *Recurvirostra avosetta,* first used in 1600 by the Italian

**📿 The avocet, "from its perpetual clamor and flippancy of tongue, is called the Lawyer," wrote Alexander Wilson.**

naturalist Ulisse Aldrovandi. This might be from *avis* (Latin for "bird"), a fondly diminutive description of the avocet, a bird of peculiar beauty and grace. In 1678 *The Ornithology of Francis Willughby* (published posthumously by Willughby's friend and collaborator John Ray) described the bird as "The Avosetta of the Italians." Its harsh cry is less bewitching than its appearance, and in Dutch the avocet is *kluut,* in imitation of this. In northern England they were also called "clickers" (because they sometimes click their bills) and "awl-birds."

The awl-shaped beak is swept from side to side to collect food from the bottom of ponds. Avocets often feed in stagnant water, and consequently are very prone to tapeworms. The famous nineteenth-century ornithologist Alexander Wilson described an avocet he took as "infested with tape-worms and a number of smaller bot-like worms."

Wilson also wrote that the avocet, "from its perpetual clamor and flippancy of tongue, is called by the inhabitants of Cape May, the Lawyer." It is rather tempting to connect this with the Latin stem *avocatio*, "a diversion," the origin of the French *avocat*, "Lawyer." But there seems to be no traceable link here, and, regretfully, we must relinquish the "flippancy of tongue" required to make one!

# BIRD OF PARADISE

It might seem that birds of paradise were deservedly named for their beautiful plumage. Instead the name more likely comes from a sixteenth-century misperception that they had no wings or feet with which to fly or perch, and therefore floated ethereally in the heavens.

When dried skins of birds of paradise were first brought to Europe from New Guinea, they were described as being without feet or wings. Such was the way they were used in New Guinea for decoration. But Europeans, who had never tried this way of preserving birds, assumed that the dried skins were complete.

The first skins from New Guinea were brought to Madrid by Juan Sebastián de Elcano, who had taken over the *Vittoria* after its first commander, Ferdinand Magellan, was killed. Elcano took the ship to the Moluccas, arriving at the island of Tidore in

November 1521. The sultan of Batjan presented the crew with skins for the king of Spain. When asked how the birds managed without wings or feet, the sultan reputedly replied that they were *manuk dewata,* or "Birds of the Gods," a name still reflected in the genus of some paradise birds, *Manucodia.*

🐦 **The name comes from a sixteenth-century misperception that these birds had no wings or feet and floated ethereally in the heavens.**

Linnaeus's name for the great bird of paradise, *Paradisaea apoda,* means "without feet" (Greek *a,* "without," and *pous,* "feet"), although by his time the birds were no longer thought footless. The name "paradise," or heaven, is from the Persian *paradeisos,* meaning an enclosed garden, which was what heaven was supposed to be.

For a long time European naturalists had speculated on the behavior of birds of paradise, concluding that after mating in the air, the female laid her eggs in a hollow on the male's back. His spectacular wiry tail was intended, they thought, to secure her while she incubated the eggs. It was also useful for tethering him to a tree when he wanted to stop floating. The name *Cicinnurus,* used for several birds of paradise, comes from the Greek *kikinnes,* "ringlet," and describes this curious curling tail.

It was not until the nineteenth century that European natural-

birds' peculiar bellowing cries. *Botaurus* comes from the Latin *butire,* "to cry" (which also gives us "bittern"), and *taurus,* "a bull."

The name *Ixobrychus* (from the Greek *ixos,* "reed," and *brukho,* "roar") was devised in 1828 by Gustav Johann Billberg, a Swedish naturalist (for whom a popular houseplant, the billbergia, was named). Bitterns have learned an extraordinary protective strategy. They can "freeze," with their bills pointing directly upward and their striped bodies exactly matching the reeds surrounding them. Sometimes if there is a breeze they even sway a little

**Sometimes called "belcher-squelchers," they seemed to be calling, "Slug-toot, slug-toot, slug-toot," wrote Thoreau.**

to imitate their reedy camouflage. "This was its instinct," wrote Thoreau, "whether it implies any conscious artifice or not."

# BLACKBIRD

Those four and twenty blackbirds baked in a pie were European blackbirds, which are a kind of thrush, not American blackbirds. Thrushes were considered a delicacy fit to "set before a king," and indeed are still eaten in some parts of the world. Although in one seventeenth-century English cookbook blackbirds were considered "better to delight the eare with their musicke than to feed the belly," in 1861 the famous Mrs. Beeton was still recommending "one blackbird to every two persons" in a recipe.

New World blackbirds were never a delicacy even though the scientific name of two of them is *Euphagus,* meaning in Greek "good to eat." American blackbirds are not related to their European namesake. They are in the Emberizidae family, and are known as Icterids which include grackles and New World orioles.

The name of the red-winged blackbird, familiar in the New

World, is *Agelaius phoeniceus*. This comes from the Greek *agelaios*, "gregarious," because these birds congregate in large flocks, except when raising their young. *Phoeniceus* is Latin for "red" (*see* Flamingo). The red "wings" are actually small patches on the male bird's shoulders, which he uses to attract females and advertise breeding territory, a strategy similar to the confident warning statement once made by bright red military uniforms. Icterids share an important characteristic called "gaping," a way of using their bills to wedge apart places where food might be hidden. A redwing blackbird will flip over a stone to find food by opening its bill under one side of the stone, causing it to roll over.

The group of birds formerly classified as a family, the Icteridae, gets its name from the Greek *ikteros,* meaning "yellow"

**In 1861 the famous Mrs. Beeton still recommended "one blackbird to every two persons" in her cookbook.**

or "jaundiced," referring to the color of European orioles, which *aren't* Icterids (*see* Oriole)! And if blackbirds aren't confusing enough, the old name for the European blackbird was the Anglo-Saxon *osle,* or Shakespeare's "ouzel-cock so black of hue." This is retained in the modern German for blackbird, *Amsel.* The English name ouzel is now used for another thrush, the ring ouzel and for the American dipper. Noted for its whistling song, the European blackbird also went by the old name of "merle." "Upon his

2797-9308

dulcet pipe the merle doth only play," wrote Shakespeare's contemporary Michael Drayton in "A Warwickshire Morning." The poet explained in a note, "Of all the birds only the blackbird whistleth."

Perhaps Wallace Stevens was inadvertently making an ornithological as well as a poetic statement when he reminded us that there are clearly more than a dozen ways of looking at a blackbird, for ornithologists as well as poets and bakers.

# BLUEBIRD

E ven in the early 1900s the idea of a "bluebird" was still sufficiently magical in Europe to be the theme of Maurice Maeterlinck's morally approbative play in which two children, searching for the "Blue Bird of Happiness," are warned, "It seems likely that the Blue Bird does not exist, or that he changes colour when he is caged."

In America bluebirds were familiar but still romanticized. The popular nineteenth-century American naturalist John Burroughs described a bluebird as a "disembodied voice; a rumor in the air . . . before it takes visible shape before you," revealing in its plumage "one of the primary hues, and the divinest of them all." Blue is traditionally the color of heaven, as well as of the Virgin Mary's robe. No wonder a bird so celestially saturated seemed mystical.

The American bluebirds, or *Sialia*s, get their name from the Greek *sialis,* meaning (not very interestingly) "a kind of bird." Unique to North America, they are members of the Turdidae, or thrush, family. There are three species: the western, mountain, and well-loved eastern bluebird, which, with its ruddy breast, re-minded early settlers of the robin redbreast back home, and was sometimes called the "blue redbreast."

Like robins, eastern bluebirds often live near houses. If short of their natural nesting sites in hollow trees, they'll use man-made cavities. Their eggs, like those of other birds that nest in dark places, never had to evolve protective markings as camouflage, and are clear pale blue or white. The parent birds return to the same nesting site each year and often lay a second clutch after the first has hatched.

**♫ Bluebirds return to the same nesting site each year.**

Early ornithologists praised bluebirds unstintingly. "No bird in Sweden," wrote the botanist Peter Kalm in the eighteenth century, "has so shiny and deep a blue as this one." William Bartram described its "most endearing warblings," as well as the male's "eagerness to please and secure the favor of his beloved female." In 1808 Alexander Wilson, a great artist and ornithologist but perhaps less good versifier, wrote a long poem (unsurprisingly not much quoted) in appreciation of the bluebird:

> He flits through the orchard, he visits each tree, . . .
> He snaps up destroyers wherever they be, . . .
> He drags the vile grub from the corn it devours . . .
> His song and his services freely are ours.

There are still many bluebird lovers. They have their own North American Bluebird Society, which publishes a journal, *Sialia*. Hundreds of Americans provide nesting boxes for bluebirds, taking care that the entrance hole is only one and a half inches in diameter (or else the bluebirds won't use it). But if all goes well they will return every year. Their spring message and lovely plumage—"With the earth tinge on his breast and the sky tinge on his back," wrote John Burroughs—is surely enough attainable happiness for one small bird to deliver.

# BOBWHITE

The bobwhite, native to America, is called a "quail" by Northerners and a "partridge" by Southerners, but although similar to both, it is neither. The name "bobwhite" is an imitation of its mating cry; some farmers, however, interpret the call as "more wet" and associate the bobwhite with coming rain. Its scientific name, *Colinus virginianus,* is from the Spanish *colin,* which in turn comes from *zolin,* a Nahuatl Indian word for "partridge." *Colin* means a quail in Mexico. *Virginianus* strictly means from the state of Virginia (named for the so-called "virgin" Queen of England, Elizabeth I), but these birds are by no means limited to Virginia.

In Virginia and elsewhere bobwhites were described by early settlers as numerous. "On going a little way," wrote Swedish traveler Peter Kalm in 1757, "you meet with great coveys of them." In *Letters from an American Farmer* (published soon after the American Revolution), Hector St. John de Crèvecoeur described feeding them and sprinkling chaff on the snow "to prevent their tender feet from freezing too fast to the earth as I have frequently observed them to do."

Like other ground birds, bobwhites prefer running to flying. They usually sleep "together in a heap," observed Kalm, arranging themselves in a compact circle with their tails inward and heads facing outward, pressing the circle tightly as each bird arrives for the night. This conserves heat and enables them to keep an all-round watch for predators. If they are disturbed, the sleeping circle will explode. The eggs in a bobwhite's nest are arranged in a similar pattern and are very tapered at one end, so they can be tightly packed. Bobwhite chicks are precocial; the eggs hatch at about the same time, and

**The name "bobwhite" is an imitation of its mating cry, although some farmers interpret the sound as "more wet" and associate the bird with coming rain.**

the downy chicks are immediately able to leave the nest, although their parents show them where to find food. One brood will include about a dozen chicks. Some are soon taken by predators. And those that do grow up often become meals for humans.

# BUNTING

E ven a simplistic endeavor to sort bird names will find buntings a challenge. *True* buntings apparently originated in South America, spreading northward and then east to Eurasia and Africa. They are common in Britain. Their English name was probably from "buntyle" in Old English ("buntlin" in Scots), which describes their plump shape. A plump, cuddly baby bundled up was also affectionately called a "bunting," as in the nursery rhyme "Bye, Baby Bunting."

As often happens, the name came back to America without necessarily referring to the same bird. Buntings are closely related to American (but not Old World) sparrows, and many birds we call sparrows in America are really buntings (*see* Sparrow). Buntings are in the Emberizidae family. However, some birds commonly *called* "buntings" in North America are in the cardinal family. These include the painted, indigo, and lazuli buntings.

The painted bunting is *Passerina ciris. Passerina* means "little sparrow" (and no, it's not a sparrow!). *Ciris,* or *keiros,* was a bird into which the Greek princess Scylla was transformed when she was about to drown, swimming after King Minos's boat when he spurned her. Scylla was the daughter of Nisus, the king of Megara, whose city was besieged by Minos. She spotted the enemy king from the battlements, fell heavily for him, and stole her father's purple lock of hair (which was magically protecting the city), to win him. Minos, although delighted with this hirsute victory, was turned off by the treacherous Scylla herself. The male painted bunting is gaudily "painted" in brilliant red and green and has, as well, a violet-blue head. The story of the purple lock was apparently enough of a connection with the bird's head for Linneaus to name it after Scylla.

> ♫ **"Bunting" describes their plump shape, like that of the bundled baby in the nursery rhyme "Bye, Baby Bunting."**

The Indigo bunting is *P. cyanea,* or "blue," which describes the male's brilliant blue color, like that of the plant dye indigo, once commonly used to dye clothes blue. The male lazuli bunting's back and head are the azure color of lapis lazuli, and its Latin name, *P. amoena,* simply means "lovely." Sometimes indigo and lazuli buntings will interbreed.

Unlike these cardinal buntings, the little American juncos *are* buntings. In his *Birds of Colonial America,* completed in 1747, Mark Catesby called the junco a "Snow bird," which is why Linnaeus named the dark-eyed junco *Junco hyemalis* (the Greek *hyemalis* means "winter"). With dark gray backs and white bellies, like bright snow under leaden skies, they are often seen in groups at bird feeders. *Junco* means "rush" in Latin, and Linnaeus may have given them this name because some European buntings live among reeds, although juncos prefer woody to rushy habitats.

One of the most common European buntings is the vividly citrine yellowhammer, *Emberiza citrinella*. Its common name has nothing to do with hammering but describes its color. Its Old English name was *amer* (amber) or *yelambre* (yellow amber).

One might think that bunting cloth, used to make flags, would have some connection with these sometimes showy little birds. But the cloth got its name from "bonting," or sifting, flour through its loose weave. Even if buntings, like flags and most other passerines, flutter, we can't connect them neatly.

# CAPERCAILLIE

The capercaillie, which lives in Scotland and northern Europe, is a very large grouse. It inhabits upland pine forests, eating mostly pine needles. Although its diet sometimes makes its flesh taste like turpentine (which also comes from pine trees), the capercaillie was once a popular game bird. To remove the taste, one old "recipe" suggested, after being soaked, buried for twenty-four hours, roasted, and steamed, the bird should then be "given to the dog, if he will eat it, for nobody else could."

In the old days it was not considered unsporting to shoot a

capercaillie perched in a tree, where it was easily taken because it concentrates so hard on its mating call that it closes its eyes. Male capercaillies are extremely jealous of their hens, and the Swiss naturalist Konrad Gesner called the capercaillie a "capricalze" in his 1554 *Historia animalium*. Probably, he derived this from *capra*, "goat," and *calcitro*," "kick," describing the cock's spirited defense of his harem. Another derivation could be the Gaelic *capullcoille,* meaning "a horse of the woods," or *cabhar coille,* an "old man" of the woods.

♫ **The sixteenth-century name "capricalze" was from the Latin for a "kicking goat" and probably referred to the male's spirited defense of his harem.**

By the eighteenth century the bird had been hunted to extinction in Scotland, and in 1837 it was reintroduced from Sweden. But pine forests continued to decrease, as the highlands of Scotland were burned annually, partly to increase the heather in which other game birds and animals feed and nest. Even if expanses of heather mean Scotland itself to some people, too much of it will soon surely oust the Old Man of the Woods forever.

# CARDINAL

**E**arly settlers simply called the northern cardinal, which is unique to North America, "the Red Bird." It was frequently captured and put in cages, where both males and females would sing "exceedingly sweet," unless "they would die with grief," wrote eighteenth-century naturalist Peter Kalm.

Our common northern cardinal, *Cardinalis cardinalis,* was originally *Loxia cardinalis. Loxos,* Greek for "crossroads" (so "cross-wise" or "crooked"), was for its curved conical beak which the cardinal uses to crush grains and seeds, rather than peeling them, as weaker-billed birds must. The name "cardinal" comes from the officials of the Catholic church, who traditionally wore bright red, a sign of affluence and power. Before synthetic dyes, red was an expensive color to obtain because it was derived from the rare cochineal insect. Consequently, only the elite could afford red garments. These influential ecclesiastics got *their* name from the Latin *cardo,* or "hinge." The balance of important ideas often "hinged" on the judgment of powerful church officials, and indeed sins or virtues could become "cardinal" too.

The cardinal family grouping has been changed several times, and it still isn't always consistent. Cardinals are now generally grouped with grosbeaks (from the French *gros,* "large," and *bec,* "beak") and buntings. The family name is Cardinalidae.

**2. The cardinal was the first bird to be given official state recognition when, in 1926, it was designated as the state bird of Kentucky.**

Older books may call the cardinal *Richmondena cardinalis,* after Charles Wallace Richmond, who spent most of his life working in Washington. He had become interested in birds when, at the age of thirteen, he was a page in the House of Representatives and was allowed access to books in the Library of Congress. While studying for a degree in medicine, he took a job as a night watchman at the United States National Museum, and gradually advanced until he became assistant curator, remaining there until he died in 1932. Although he made a card index of all the known birds and was greatly appreciated by his contemporaries, he is not much recognized these days.

His former namesake, however, was the first bird in the United States to be given official state recognition when, in 1926, it was designated as the state bird of Kentucky. Now it's the bird of seven states. This peak of avian hierarchy is (nomenclatorially speaking) an unclear separation of church and state—but, as yet, unchallenged.

# CHAFFINCH

Chaffinches were sometimes called "bachelor birds" because they often congregate in flocks of one sex, and their scientific name, *Fringilla coelebs,* comes from *caelebs,* Latin for "unmarried." The "chaff" part of their name derives from the Middle English *chaefen,* "to warm," referring either to the warm, rosy color of their breast or to chaff they find and eat in barnyards, which they frequent.

All three species of chaffinches are found in Eurasia, where they are among the most common birds. The "finch" part of their name, *finc* in Anglo-Saxon, is now applied to many small seed-eating birds. Much of what we know about birdsong has been learned from the study of chaffinches. As early as the eighteenth century, the German baron Johann Ferdinand Adam von Pernau, a pioneering student of bird behavior and field investigation, experimented with young chaffinches on his estate at Rosenau. Pernau believed that if man studied nature, admiration of "God's creatures" would "soon diminish the evils of the world, including "the devilish masquerades, the vain and often riduculous pomp, nay even the bloody wars." He watched birds and marked them (by cutting off one toe), and he exposed young chaffinches to the songs of tree pipits which the chaffinches then imitated. Pernau refused to "hunt after honors" by putting his name on the books he wrote—which remained anonymous for two hundred years!

Chaffinches' songs can change "dialect" over quite small distances where breeding groups are separated by open meadows. It seems that the males inherit a basic song pattern, but they learn particular refinements and flourishes by listening to other males before sexual maturity, after which their song be-

♪ **Chaffinches were sometimes called "bachelor birds" because they often congregate in flocks of one sex.**

comes fixed. This gives the species members basic recognition of one another, which is essential for communication, but also allows for song variations to define territory.

The means of obtaining some of this information has included raising chaffinches in total isolation, deafening them at various stages of their development, and injecting them with hormones. One is somewhat reminded of the emperor Frederick II (1194–1250), who "wanted to discover what language a child would use when he grew up if he had never heard anyone speak." His experimental raising of babies in isolation, without being spoken to or fondled, was "in vain, because all of the infants died." He no doubt thought these experiments no odder than we do when we manipulate the lives and bodies of birds in the cause of science. Our descendants, however, may think otherwise.

# Coot

A
lthough a twelfth-century bestiary claimed that a coot
will care for abandoned eaglets "with the same mater-
nal zeal she shows for her own offspring," from our
point of view she is a hard-hearted mother. Coots lay large
clutches of eggs but end up with few chicks. They selectively feed
their young: in America the chicks who beg most vociferously are
fed; in Europe the parent coots will actually shake a chick to
death if it is too demanding.

Coots make nests on the water, anchored to reeds, and the
chicks swim as soon as they hatch. They have only partially

webbed feet, with lobed toes, but can dive deep; when wounded, a coot will sometimes dive down and cling to bottom weeds.

They are sometimes called "black ducks" or "mud hens," but coots are actually related to rails. Rails don't have lobed toes, but some of them have very long toes, so they can stand on lily pads. Although coots congregate in open water, most rails are shy, hiding in marshes. The name "rail" comes from the Old French *raille,* "rattle," which is the sound they make when hiding. The modern French *râle* means both the bird and a rattle, especially a death-rattle. Rails can compress their bodies to slip through very narrow gaps between reeds, making themselves "as thin as a rail."

> These birds, with partly white heads, were once called "baldicootes."

Alexander Wilson did not distinguish between coots, rails, and soras. He said sportsmen found "this bird . . . an inexplicable mystery," because "it comes they know not whence; and goes they know not where." We know now that some American coots migrate to South America. In Britain coots don't usually migrate.

Coots are found worldwide. The American coot is *Fulica americana,* from the Latin *fuligo,* "soot." The European coot is *F. atra* because coots are black. *Atra* is from Latin *ater,* "black."

When hunters go "cooting" they are pursuing not coots but other waterbirds, usually sea ducks or scoters (whose name may come from their "sooty" plumage, similar to a coot's). Neither scoters nor coots taste very good in spite of the popularity of "cooting," a verb originally coined in the seventeenth century for the copulation of turtles, sometimes called "cooters."

The bird's name "coot" is supposedly imitative of their cry. These birds, with their partly white heads, were once called "baldicootes," and we still describe people being "as bald as a coot." However "coot" is most used to describe a silly person— with or without a bald pate.

# CORMORANT

S atan, in John Milton's *Paradise Lost,* "sat like a cormorant" on the Tree of Life, watching Adam and Eve and "devising death." Real cormorants, with snakelike necks, perch eerily on trees too, spreading their dark wings to dry.

Cormorants soak their plumage to reduce buoyancy before sinking underwater in search of prey. They dive deep down from the surface of the water, propelled by their feet, and emerge to eat their catch. Their vestigial nostrils are permanently closed, and above water they breathe through their mouths.

Adult cormorants are partly or wholly black, with a glossy plumage that can reflect many hues. Their common name comes from the Latin *corvus marinus,* or "raven of the sea." Their family is the Phalacrocoracidae, from the Greek *phalakros,* "bald," and *korax,* "raven." They don't have bald heads, although some have white on their heads or faces, which probably gave them this name.

Some cormorants are called shags (from the Icelandic *skegg*, "beard") and have shaggy tufts of nuptial head plumes. The names are often used interchangeably. Although the Australian expression "like a shag on a rock" means being in an isolated position, cormorants are generally rather gregarious. In Scotland they were also called scarts, or scarfs, from the Old Norse *skarfr,* imitative of their harsh cry.

Cormorants have all four toes webbed, a characteristic called totipalmate. They use their large feet to keep their eggs warm, because they have no bare brood patch on the abdomen, as most birds do. They fly well, except for the flightless Galápagos cormorant, *Phalacrocorax harrisi,* named after Charles Harris, a nineteenth-century naturalist in the Galápagos, who should not be confused with Audubon's friend Edward

♎ **Satan, in Milton's** *Paradise Lost,* **"sat like a cormorant" on the Tree of Life, watching Adam and Eve and "devising death."**

Harris (*see* Hawk). Its former name (still sometimes used) was *Nannopterum harrisi,* from the Greek *nanos,* "dwarf," and *pterum,* "wing." This cormorant doesn't even have the keeled breastbone of most birds, which is where the flight muscles are attached.

In Asia, tame cormorants have been trained for centuries to hunt fish. A ring or cord around the neck prevents them from swallowing their catch. In Britain, the Stuart king James adopted this practice, and in 1611 paid John Wood, master of cormorants, thirty pounds for training "certain fowls called cormorants" and "making them fit for the use of fishing." More recently, in 1979, a study of fishermen's cormorants on the Li-chiang River described a tradition of loosening the ring around the bird's neck after seven fish so it could catch the eighth for itself. Apparently the cormorants invariably stopped fishing after the seventh fish— suggesting that they could keep numerical count of their catch!

# COWBIRD

Williliam Swainson, who contributed much to ornithology but was not a scholar, named the brown-headed cowbird *Molothrus ater,* thinking he was calling it by the Greek for "parasite," *molobrus.* In accordance with the complicated rules of nomenclature, this mistake remains permanent. *Ater* means "black."

Swainson was Audubon's friend but misjudgedly refused to collaborate on the *Birds of America* because, he said, Audubon intended to "conceal my name—and transfer my fame to your papers and reputation." His "fame" was not long lasting, nor was the natural system he championed, which formed curious biological connections, such as relating penguins to turtles.

Brown-headed cowbirds originally followed the American bison, scavenging food in soil kicked by their hooves and pecking insects off their backs. Rare in the Northeast until colonization, they increased along with domestic cattle. In the eighteenth century Mark Catesby described "Cowpen" birds that "delight much to feed in the pens of cattle, which has given them their name."

Cowbirds are obligate parasites, which are unable to build their own nests and raise their own young. They rely on other birds to do so, monitoring the prospective host's nest building before depositing an egg of their own. Nonobligate parasites only sometimes rely on foster parents. The beginning of avian parasitism has long been fodder for scientific speculation. When cowbirds were nomadic, following bison herds for food, they may have started depending on other birds to raise their young. In 1874, however, the famous ornithologist Elliot Coues vividly imagined another possible origin of this curious habit. A cowbird, he postulated, "in imminent danger of [egg] delivery without a nest prepared . . . loth to lose her offspring . . . deposited her burthen in an alien nest. . . . The convenience of this process may have struck her." One can almost imagine her deciding to pursue a fulfilling career. Coues, incidentally, married three times.

The cowbird's egg has a very short incubation period (eleven days), so the fledgling often hatches before its host siblings, then grows with phenomenal rapidity, getting an unfair share of food. Although the cowbird may destroy some of the host's eggs, some

🎵 "Cowpen" birds, wrote Mark Catesby, "delight much to feed in the pens of cattle, which has given them their name."

of the host's own young usually survive, and in Panama there is even a cowbird whose fledglings remove lethal botfly larvae from host siblings. Generally, however, hosts do not benefit from parasitism, and some birds, notably robins and catbirds, recognize the alien eggs and destroy them. Smaller birds, like the yellow warbler, with "surprising ingenuity," as Thomas Brewer wrote to his friend Audubon, build another nest on top of the parasitized one. Brewer sent Audubon a three-storied nest (they can be up to six stories!).

Young cowbirds inherit an amazing ability to recognize their own species, and even if they mature without seeing another cowbird, they respond to and congregate with their kind, knowing where to migrate together after the adult birds have left. Other birds need to be taught recognition and migratory routes but have innate instincts not shared by the cowbird. It's not just in birds that the connections between inheritance and learning are unresolved. Birds can be obligate or nonobligate parasites. Humans sometimes consider themselves "noblesse," but they don't necessarily "oblige."

# CRANE

I f you have a pedigree, you have a *pied de grue,* or "crane's foot." Cranes are palustral, inhabiting marshes, and although they spend much of their time in shallow water, they do not have webbed feet. A crane's foot was a symbol used to denote succession in a genealogical tree, with a main stem and toes branching off, and it came to be associated with a long and illustrious lineage.

Cranes themselves have an ancient lineage and dwelt in prehistoric marshes before humanity had yet emerged. By the Bronze Age our ancestors were eating them, and the name "crane" goes back to an Indo-European root, *gar* or *kar,* "to cry out." Their haunting, gutteral cry comes from their immensely long trachea (over a yard in length), which is curled around behind their breastbone like a trombone. When mating, they will sing duets, and the flock cries in unison when landing or taking off. Cranes are found all over the world except South America and Antarctica and seem to have been revered by humans everywhere. In Japan they were called "marsh gods."

Cranes get airborne by running against the wind, and they keep aloft with a heavy, upstroking wingbeat (in other birds the downstroke is more powerful). Unlike storks, which cranes resemble, they roost and nest on the ground, and the fledglings grow their long legs rapidly in about two weeks; the wings grow later. When roosting, cranes tuck one leg up under their feathers to keep it warm and stand on the other. In the Middle Ages it was believed that a sentinel crane held a stone in one foot, which would drop if it dozed or if its attention wandered, thus waking its companions. That's why in heraldry a crane is often shown holding a stone, as a reminder of alertness.

**♌ If you have a pedigree, you have a *pied de grue,* or "crane's foot."**

But cranes don't stand still much except when sleeping, and they get most of their food by busily searching for it. Their vigorous and incredible mating dances have been imitated in many cultures. Plutarch described Theseus and his companions celebrating their victory over the Minotaur with a dance, "imitative of the windings and twistings of the labyrinth," subsequently called the "crane dance."

Most cranes are at least partly migratory, flying in wedge formation and following a leader that medieval observers called their captain. The migratory route has to be taught to a chick (sometimes two chicks) by its parents, who stay with it until it can fly. The parents themselves stay with each other for life—and for the Japanese that made cranes a symbol of marital happiness, often depicted on kimonos. "One thousand cranes" is a wish for good luck, longevity, and happiness, multiplied one thousand times.

# CROW

Crows are everywhere, even in our language. The scarecrow, especially Dorothy's friend in *The Wizard of Oz,* is familiar to the smallest children, although they probably don't associate him with the bird at all. Adults using crowbars don't think of the crow's strong curved bill, which, like the tool it names, is designed to pry loose and turn heavy objects. When we search around our eyes for crow's-feet we are more likely worrying about aging than remembering the characteristic tracks in snow or mud left by walking crows.

Crows build bulky nests high in trees, and sailors scanned the horizon from a crow's nest too. Real crows' nests are so roughly built that sticks often drop to the ground during their construction. In the eighteenth century Gilbert White, in his *Natural History and Antiquities of Selbourne,* said that the poor relied on the sticks dropped by crows for fuel, since landlords kept most available wood for themselves. In America wood was plentiful for everyone, but there was still discrimination in the form of "Jim Crow" laws. Jim Crow was a black stable hand who hummed to himself while dancing; he gave his name to the song "Jump, Jim Crow," and then to a racist attitude.

> ♫ When we search for crow's-feet around our eyes, we are more likely worrying about aging than remembering the tracks left by walking crows.

The crow, or Corvidae, family includes crows, ravens, rooks, choughs, jays, and jackdaws, many of which are wholly or partly black. The name Corvidae comes from the Latin *corvus,* "a crow." The American common crow is very similar to the Eurasian carrion crow, and most crows eat carrion. The hooded crow, a gray bird with a black head, gets its Scottish name, corbie, from *corbeau,* a French word for "crow." In the ghoulish seventeenth-century Scottish ballad "Twa' Corbies," two hooded crows gleefully discuss dining on the body of a knight and pecking out his "bonny blue e'en," a common habit of corvids (*see* Raven).

Crows are most often associated with corpses and dark death, although the chough, common in Cornwall, was said to be the spirit of the legendary hero King Arthur. Their voices, far from being heavenly, are harsh and unmusical, even though corvids are passerines, that is, perching or "song" birds. "Crow" comes from the Anglo-Saxon *crawe,* an imitation of their cry, although nowadays roosters "crow" and crows "caw," without an *r.* The rook, a kind of Eurasian crow, gets its English name from the Old Norse *hrokr,* describing a hoarse unlovely voice. The rook's scientific name is *Corvus frugilegus,* meaning "fruit gathering crow," although rooks mostly eat (to us) less appetizing fare.

Crows and their relatives are considered the world's most highly developed and adaptable birds. They are abundant almost all over the world. They were so common that before the advent of clocks, if the sky was overcast and the sunset was obscured, Hebrews would begin their Sabbath when crows came to roost at sunset, traveling "as straight as a crow flies." Mostly, though, we take little heed of crows flying through our lives and our language. We don't even find them palatable — and, indeed, "eating crow" is apt to stick in one's throat.

# Cuckoo

All over Europe the distinctive call was a sign that the cuckoo had returned from wintering in Africa and spring had arrived. "Sing cucu, nu. Sing cuccu, / Sumer is i-cumen in," goes the earliest ballad in the English language.

The American yellow-billed cuckoo doesn't have the typical cuckoo cry. Its name is *Coccyzus americanus,* from the Greek *kokkuzo,* meaning "I cry cuckoo" (even though it doesn't). The black-billed cuckoo is *C. erythrophthalmus,* from *erythros,* "red," and *opthalmos,* "eye," because it has a red ring around its eye.

Even if Americans aren't familiar with the cuckoo's actual call they often know how it sounds from cuckoo clocks. These were invented, in a small Black Forest village, in about 1740, by Franz Anton Ketterer. He cleverly used bellows to reproduce the cuckoo's characteristic two-note call. This cry is imitated in the bird's common name, which came to Britain from the Old

French *cucu.* The scientific name, *Cuculus canorus,* means "a melodious cuckoo," from the Latin *canere,* "to sing."

It was known from Aristotle's time that the European cuckoo lays her eggs in the nests of other birds. A French tradition connecting cuckoos with adultery had reached Britain by the time of Shakespeare, who wrote in *Love's Labour's Lost* that the cuckoo's song "mocks married men." The husband of an unfaithful wife is a "cuckold."

The real cuckoo's cuckoldry is no game of love but a demanding survival strategy. The mother cuckoo closely watches a nest until its owners are absent. She must quickly remove (and usually eat) the hosts' eggs and deposit her own single egg, which has an extra-thick shell so that she won't break it in her haste. Because

**The cuckoo's song "mocks married men," wrote Shakespeare; the husband of an unfaithful wife is a "cuckold."**

the hosts often eject the strange egg, the cuckoo may lay twenty eggs in twenty different nests to be sure a few survive. Remarkably, many of these eggs match those of their host, even though different cuckoos parasitize different birds. If there are any of its foster parents' eggs or chicks still in the nest when the young cuckoo hatches, it scoops them out, using a special hollow in its back. The foster parents, once they have initially accepted the egg, take no notice of this murderous practice, caring for their cuckoo devotedly, even if it grows so big it can't fit the nest. The foster mother, says a seventeenth-century translation of Pliny, "joyeth to see so goodly a bird . . . and wonders at herself that she hath hatched and reared so trim [meaning fine] a chick." The grown chick knows where to migrate and with what bird to mate, even if it has never seen another cuckoo.

Cuckoos are found worldwide, linked by characteristics such as zygodactyl feet (two toes face forward, two back), but only about a third of them are parasitic. The two North American cuckoos aren't parasitic, but they aren't skilled nest builders; like European cuckoos, they are shy woodland birds that arrive from the south in spring to breed.

To be "cuckoo" also means to be crazy. The cuckoo's way of life is certainly not as traditionally domesticated as that of many birds, but most probably the connection comes from its importunate, crazy voice in the giddy season of spring.

# CURLEW

Curlews are known for their haunting cry and their sickle-shaped bills, described in their generic name, *Numenius,* from the Greek *neos mene,* meaning "new moon." This long, downward-curving bill is used for probing deep into mud and sand. Opening it underground would require enormous lateral force, so the curlew's remarkable bill has evolved to open at its tip only, a quality called rhynchokinensis. The movable joints of its upper jaw are in front of the skull and push the upper bill forward, so the tip, which even has tactile nerves, is free to move independently and can be used as delicately as a forefinger.

Curlews poke for crabs and other such food (regurgitating the indigestible parts), but they also eat insects and berries. The "curlew berries" of Newfoundland formed an important part of the Eskimo curlew's diet, before its long migration from Alaska to Argentina. As it flew south it was hunted mercilessly: In 1863, seven thousand Eskimo curlews were shot in Nantucket in *one day*. Sometimes they were so fat that they burst open when they hit the ground, exposing a doughy pad of fat on the breast, which led hunters to call them "dough birds." The Eskimo curlew is now thought to be extinct.

The bristle-thighed curlew has "bristles," or unbarbed feathers, on its thighs. It migrates six thousand miles, including eighteen hundred miles over water with no resting place, from Alaska to the Polynesian Islands. It is called *N. tahitiensis* because it was first found in Tahiti by Joseph Banks, when he voyaged around the world from 1768 to 1771 with Captain Cook. The long-billed curlew, *N. americanus,* used to be widespread over America, nesting on the prairies, but is less common these days.

*In 1863, seven thousand Eskimo curlews were shot in Nantucket in one day; some-times they were so fat that hunters called them "dough birds."*

The Eurasian, or common, curlew's name, *N. arquata,* is from the Latin *arcus,* "a bow," describing the shape of the bill. "Curlew" is thought echoic of the bird's cry, but it could come from the French *curlieu,* also meaning "courier" (*courre,* "run," and *lieu,* "place"), for curlews fly purposefully overhead, often in V formation.

The whimbrel, or Hudsonian curlew, is more common than other curlews. It was shyer of people and did not follow the same disastrous migratory routes. Whimbrels are widespread in America, Europe, and Siberia. In the sixteenth century, the whimbrel was called a "whimpernel," and it probably got its name from its "whimpering" cry, reminiscent of the whining of whelps, or puppies. Its Scottish name is "waup."

Curlews start their autumn migration just before stormy weather, crying out as they fly in darkness. Dylan Thomas described these moon-billed birds crying overhead, "under the conceiving moon." They could be lured down by hunters imitating them, then dazzled and shot by lamplight. As late as 1942, you could still buy curlews in London butcher shops for only three shillings and sixpence each. You can't buy them anymore. These days we are content if we see or hear them alive.

# DIPPER

John Muir, known by his friends as "John O'Mountains," explored the area around the Yosemite and was influential in conserving it as national parkland. He did not give his name to any bird, but his rhapsodic article for the February 1878 issue of *Scribner's Monthly* will forever associate him with the dipper, which, he wrote, "has cheered me so much in my lonely wanderings."

Muir called the dipper "the hummingbird of blooming waters," but it is related to wrens and thrushes, not hummingbirds. Dippers are in the Cinclidae family (from the Greek *kinklo*, "waterbird") and are unique among passerines, or perching birds, because, in spite of their sparrowlike feet, dippers are aquatic, swimming well and diving deep. They waterproof their outer feathers with oil, from a preen gland that is ten times bigger than a sparrow's. They can close their nostrils with special flaps, and a membrane protects their eyes underwater.

Their common name most probably describes a habit of bobbing up and down on their legs when out of the water, but dippers also dip or dive into streams. They bob in and out of rocky, fast-flowing streams, seeming to discern no difference between water and land, and counteracting their buoyancy by clinging with their claws to the stream bed. When a dipper swims or walks underwater, propelled and steadied by its short wings, it leans forward into the current so that the water deflects upward, "in the form of a clear, crystalline shell, which fairly incloses him like a bell-glass," said Muir.

Another name for the dipper is the water ouzel. Around the seventeenth century, the name "ouzel" was transferred from blackbirds to dippers (*see* Blackbird). In Scotland, dippers were sometimes called water piets because of their sooty brown-and-white "pied" plumage. The

*♫* **John Muir wrote that dippers "sing water songs, for they hear them all their lives, and even before they are born."**

Eurasian dipper is *Cinclus cinclus,* and the two New World species of dippers, *C. mexicanus* and *C. leucocephalus* ("white-headed"), live in the western and southern mountain ranges. The Asian brown dipper is *C. pallasii*, named after a German naturalist, Peter Pallas, who explored Siberia for the Russian empress Catherine the Great. Linnaeus called him "a most acute young man" (although Pallas had boldly criticized Linnaeus's classification of worms!). Pallas was one of the first scientists to adopt Linnaeus's binomial system.

When dippers fly any distance, they never cross land but

follow streams. Their domed nests are of soft green moss with an arched opening. Dippers always nest near water, in crevices of rocks, sometimes behind waterfalls. As Muir wrote (better than anyone ever could again), they "sing water songs, for they hear them all their lives, and even before they are born."

# Duck

We are likely to encounter ducks before we can even speak. They float in our infant bathtubs; they decorate our bibs at mealtimes; we are taken to feed them for a treat; they animate our earliest literature. Ducks have been part of human lives for a long time, both as cheerful symbols and as meals. The ancient Egyptians (who did not know chickens) portrayed wild ducks on their friezes. The Chinese domesticated ducks four thousand years ago, and both they and the Romans knew how to hatch the eggs in incubators.

Although in the popular song the ill-fated Clementine thought it necessary to drive ducklings to the water "every morning, just at nine," domestic ducks can live on land as long as they have plenty to drink. Indeed, farm ducklings hatched without mothers can sometimes drown if introduced to water too early. All

**♀ After mating, drakes molt; a "sitting duck" has lost its feathers and cannot fly.** domestic ducks, except pure Muscovys, are related to the mallards. Male ducks (drakes) are among the few birds with a penis, and sometimes their clinging ardor will drown their beloved. The name "mallard," from the Latin *masculus,* means "male." Wild mallards and domestic ducks are "dabbling," or "puddle,"

ducks. They swim on the surface but upend to feed. Diving ducks, which feed underwater and whose bodies are submerged when they swim, dive deep, paddling with both feet in unison (rather than alternately, like the dabblers).

Domestic, or "table," ducks include Long Island duckling, descended from nine Peking ducks brought there in 1873 by a Yankee clipper. Muscovy ducks probably get their name from the musky odor of their flesh. They originally came from the country of the Mysca Indians in Nicaragua; it's also possible that their name mistakenly comes from Moscow, another faraway place. The French crossbred Muscovys and mallards to obtain Barbary ducks, which have a milder taste but can't quack! Much epicurean energy has gone into duck cuisine: Chinese gourmets served the "Seventeen Ineffable Precious Parts" of the duck; French gourmets invented a "duck press," designed to squeeze out the reddish juices of Rouen ducks, strangled rather than beheaded to achieve this gustatory refinement.

The canvasback duck gets its name from a waistcoat. In the old days when cloth was expensive, waistcoats were often backed with cheaper white canvas (which didn't show under a coat). The male canvasback has a white back like such a waistcoat.

Ducks are in much of our language. The soft breast feathers used to line the eider duck's nest and harvested for quilts gave us "eiderdown" (from the Norse *aedur* and *dunn,* meaning "downbird"). After mating, a drake molts, and a "sitting duck" is one that has lost its feathers and cannot fly. The name "duck" is from the Anglo-Saxon *duce* ("diver"), from the days when the innocence of witches was tested in a "ducking pond." Ducks are everywhere, from when we first lisp "quack" and laugh at cartoons, to when there is no future left for us and we become "dead ducks."

# EAGLE

The eagle is an ancient symbol of power, often depicted fighting a serpent, the symbol of evil. In Sumeria, India, Egypt, and Mexico, gods were pictured in the form of eagles. The Roman god Jupiter became an eagle in order to abduct Ganymede, the object of his fancy.

The golden eagle is *Aquila chrysaetos,* meaning literally "eagle, golden eagle." Its neck feathers reflect light, glinting like sunshine or precious metal, and it was thought able to stare at the sun—probably because it has a transparent "nictitating membrane," or extra eyelid typical of birds of prey. The word comes from the Latin *nictare,* "to wink," as the eyelid closes instantly to protect the bird's eye. Eagles are among the longest living birds and reputedly renewed themselves eternally by flying up to the burning sun and then plunging down into the sea. Saint

John the Evangelist preached renewal through Christianity, which is why church lecterns are often in the form of an eagle, a symbol of rebirth as well as power.

Eagles have been symbols of military strength too, often depicted on army banners. In World War II the Germans called the day they were to begin their air attack on Britain *Adlertag,* or "eagle day." Both male and female eagles are exemplary parents, as well as faithful partners.

Once eagles were thought to steal infants, although the weight of a tiny newborn is about as much as most eagles can carry. However, the Philippine monkey-eating eagle, one of the largest birds in the world, with distinctive blue eyes, is a threat to quite large monkeys.

**⚲ Benjamin Franklin called the bald eagle a "bird of bad moral character."**

The bald eagle's preferred food is fish, and its name, *Haliaeetus,* comes from the Greek *halos,* "sea," and *aetos,* "eagle." The second part of its name, *leucocephalus,* means "white-headed." The white feathers on its head and neck make it appear bald; the Old English word *balde* also meant "white."

Benjamin Franklin did not want the great seal of the newly founded American nation to portray the bald eagle because of its kleptoparasitism, or habit of stealing prey from other birds. He called it a "bird of bad moral character." His first choice for the seal was a depiction of the Red Sea with "Rays from a pillar of fire . . . beaming on Moses," who is cheerfully about to cause the waters to "overflow Pharaoh." His second choice had a turkey as the avian emblem.

The American seal took from 1776 to 1782 to design, and the bald eagle won the day, carrying a conciliatory olive branch in its right talon. Our forefathers probably didn't think so, but our great national eagle may well be a female, because eagles are reversely dimorphic, the female being larger than the male. One theory for this is that females need to protect themselves from the males. Another theory, not much postulated by ornithologists, is that perhaps male eagles *like* their mates with an aquiline beak and a Junoesque build.

# EGRET

All egrets are herons, although not all herons are egrets. The name "egret" comes from the French *aigrette,* meaning a "little heron," probably derived from *haigron,* the Old German for "heron."

The cattle egret, *Bubulcus ibis,* is not an ibis, in spite of the second part of its name. *Bubulcus* is the Latin word for "ploughman," used because these birds follow grazing animals, dining on insects disturbed by their hooves. Once an Old World bird, the cattle egret is now established in America too.

The great egret is best known for its feathery nuptial plumes, or "aigrettes," which now mean the tuft of feathers as well as the bird itself. It lives in North and South America and was almost hunted to extinction in Florida. Like all members of the Ardeidae, or heron family, these egrets are devoted parents, a devotion cruelly exploited by egret hunters in the nineteenth century. Egret plumes were in great demand for ladies' hats, and greed coupled with vanity pushed the price of egret feathers to twice that of gold. In 1892, 130,000 egret "scalps" were sent to milliners in New York. Parent egrets won't leave their young even if in danger themselves. Hunters decimated rookeries, often leaving dying, scalped parent birds to rot and their nestlings to starve.

**At the turn of the twentieth century women boycotted hat feathers "in the name of motherhood."**

But at the turn of the century women boycotted hat feathers "in the name of motherhood." Protests escalated when, on July 8, 1905, Guy Bradley, a warden of Monroe County in Florida, tried to arrest egret poachers and was shot to death, leaving a wife and two small sons. During the public outcry, insurance companies canceled coverage for feather factories. In 1913, an act of Congress restricted the use of plumes on hats. Embroidered "Audubon hats" were promoted by the Audubon Society, "wherein beauty is achieved without robbing the feathered kingdom of its plumage." Like all fashions they came and went. The Audubon Society, however continued to grow, and has been protecting birds from ourselves ever since.

# EMU AND CASSOWARY

One of the early convict colonies in Australia was governed by Arthur Phillip who, in 1789, described the new strange birds he found there. He sent home illustrations, as well as a stuffed emu, which ornithologists in London called *Casuarius novaehollandiae,* or "Cassowary from New Holland." "New Holland" is an old name for Australia, from where emus come. Emus and cassowaries are closely related.

Cassowaries from northeastern Australia and Papua New Guinea were brought to Europe in the late sixteenth century. By 1676 there were enough cassowaries in Charles II's exotic bird collection in St. James's Park, and the East India Company was informed, "His Majestie desires no more Cassawarrens." This name, later replaced by "cassowary," comes from the Aboriginal word *suwari.* In 1758, Linnaeus named the cassowary *Struthio casurius,* thinking it was a kind of ostrich. *Struthio* means "ostrich."

The emu's name also meant "ostrich," coming from the Portuguese *emen,* which in turn came from the Arabic *na'amu,* "ostrich." Syrian ostriches roamed the Arabian plains before their extinction there in the early twentieth century.

Several species of emu apparently became extinct after European settlement in Australia. *Dromaius novaehollandiae* is now the only member of its family, the Dromaiidae (which means "swift running"). The emu has long legs and a fast, bouncy run. Its wings are small and hang limply, and its plumage is shaggy rather than fluffy, parting neatly down the middle of its back. Far from being extinct, *this* emu is considered an agricultural pest, and in 1932 the "Emu War" was waged against it. For a month the Australian Royal Artillery attacked twenty thousand emus with machine guns; the emus split into small groups and scattered. The guerilla tactics of the emus, as well as public outcry, put an end to the assault, but in the 1940s the Australian government was still offering a bounty of four shillings for each emu bill.

"If I were a cassowary,
On the plains
of Timbuctoo,
I would eat a
missionary,
Cassock, bands
and hymn-
book too."

Cassowaries hide in dense woods and are far less common than emus. They have thick, short legs (which can deliver a mortal blow) and a curious helmetlike casque on top of their head. This is used for bashing through brush and sifting for fallen berries and other food. The males, except for Bennett's cassowary, have bright droopy wattles on their necks.

George Bennett was an Australian naturalist with eclectic interests. In 1834 he wrote *Wanderings in New South Wales,* in which, as well as describing animals and birds, he included the observation that "the London pickpockets are considered to make the best shepherds in the colony, as it suits their naturally idle habits." His varied exertions contributed to the founding of the Sydney Botanic Garden and to bringing the skeleton of a sperm whale to the Sydney Museum, where it still remains.

Cassowaries intrigued another eminent Victorian, Samuel Wilberforce, the Anglican bishop of Oxford. "If I were a cassowary," he wrote, "On the plains of Timbuctoo, / I would eat a missionary, / Cassock, bands and hymn-book too." Wilberforce was an ardent anti-Catholic *and* an opponent of Charles Darwin. He never traveled abroad, and apparently did not know that cassowaries are from Australasia, *not* Timbuktu in Africa, where ostriches live.

# Falcon

The ancient Egyptian God Horus, lofty companion of the sun, had the head of a falcon. Falcons seem to circle near the sun, high above their prey. Then, dropping like thunderbolts, they grasp their airborne victim, stunning it and severing the cervical vertebrae with their beak. They avoid catching prey on the ground where their long, pointed wings might easily be damaged in brush.

Falcons are built for speed; even their heads are streamlined, without the bony upper brow of the hawk family, and their nostrils have a whorled air passage to break the tremendous rush of air into them as they dive.

The falcon family is Falconidae, from the Latin *falx,* "a sickle," the shape of their formidably sharp beak and taloned feet. Their wings are also sickle-shaped. In Medieval England they were called *faucons.* Later the Latin "l" was reintroduced, but not always pronounced. The surname Faulkner, pronounced without the "l," referred to someone who hunted with falcons.

At some time in prehistory men began using birds of prey as hunters. Birds, which could be trained to bring back their catch were better than arrows, which were hard to make and easy to lose. Hunting with birds, often reserved for the great and powerful, was practiced throughout ancient Arabia and Asia, but not by the Jews, who thought birds that feed on flesh would contaminate the prey and make it "unclean."

The peregrine falcon is widespread throughout the world, except for the polar regions. Unlike some falcons, it is migratory, getting its name from the Latin *per,* "through," and *ager,* "field," making *peregrinus* and meaning "wanderer." Naturalist John Ray in 1713 explained that they were so named "from passing out of one country into another." A male peregrine falcon was called a tiercel, or tercel-gentle (as in Shakespeare). This means a "third." Male peregrine falcons are about a third smaller than females, and in a nest of three young birds two are generally females and one is a male.

**The peregrine falcon's name means "wanderer," because they pass out of one country and into another.**

Diurnal birds of prey like falcons hunt during the day and become docile in darkness. Once they were tamed by "ciliation," a cruel but skillful practice of "seeling" the upward-closing eyelids by passing a thread through them and tying it to the top of the bird's head. As the bird became more docile the eyelids were gradually allowed to open. In *The Art of Hunting with Birds,* the thirteenth-century emperor Frederick II compared hunting with "inanimate objects or trained quadripeds" to the "nobler, more worthy" art of falconry. He introduced the Arabian "hood," which covered the bird's head to subdue it. Although church officials were enthusiastic falconers, the pope excommunicated Frederick for not participating in crusades against the "infidels." In fact, the emperor actually introduced some Arabian (infidel) customs into his own court, including keeping a harem, complete with eunuchs.

# FLAMINGO

Today we associate flamingos with Florida. But although they have always visited, they haven't always been residents. The birds probably were there in prehistoric times, but only in the 1930s did they *nest* in Florida again. They were introduced by Joseph E. Widener, the developer of Florida's Hialeah Race Track Park. He thought the park needed "one additional touch to make [it] a tropical Eden." Thirty flamingos that were imported from Cuba flew away, so Widener brought more every year until he finally succeeded in getting the birds to nest by dumping loads and loads of mud near them.

Flamingos' foot-high mud nests have always puzzled ornithologists. William Dampier, a colorful character, part swashbuckler, part naturalist (cruising in a pirated Danish ship renamed *Bachelor's Delight*) first wrote in 1683 that flamingos "could neither draw [their legs] very conveniently in their Nests, nor sit down upon them." He concluded that they straddled their high nests, an idea still held in the nineteenth century, when the naturalist-priest Abbé Giovanni Molina reported that flamingos nested "as if seated in a chair." In 1904 the ornithologist Frank Chapman was determined to discover the truth. Crouching behind a blind in the Bahamas, "like a spy in an enemy's camp," he finally saw that flamingos tuck their long legs under them to brood.

**The mythical phoenix was burned in flames and rose again; early Christians thought the flamingo might be a kind of phoenix.**

When Spanish explorers saw flamingos, they named them *flamenco,* from the Latin *flamma,* "flame." The fiery Spanish Gypsy "flamenco" music is not related. It meant "Flemish" (for where Gypsies were thought to have come from).

The American or West Indian flamingo is *Phoenicopterus ruber.* It is brighter than its relatives in southern Europe, Asia, Africa, and Central America.

*Phoenicopterus ruber* is from the Phoenicians, who were famous for their use of red (in Latin, *rubus*) dye. The name could also come from the mythical phoenix, which was burned in flames and rose again. Early Christians thought the flamingo might be a kind of phoenix and noticed, too, that in flight, with its legs extended and wings spread out, it made the figure of a cross.

Related to avocets, not geese, as was once thought, flamingos congregate in the thousands, often in isolated places, where they feed in briny, caustic water that other creatures avoid. Their bright yellow legs and stunning red, pink, and coral feathers are colored by the carotenoids in their food. If they are deprived of the necessary canthaxanthin, their feathers will fade to white. Initially this disappointed the keepers of flamingos in captivity, until someone thought of including carrots or beets in their diet.

Their normal food includes shrimp and algae, which they extract from mud or surface water, according to the shape of their bills. With their heads upside down they turn in circles, sieving nutrients through their bills and pumping out water with their large tongues. These thick tongues are very oily, and were considered a delicacy by Roman epicures.

For such strange individuals their use as croquet mallets in Alice's Wonderland doesn't seem odd. Fittingly, Alice holds hers upside down, its "knees" bent forward, in an accurate but fantastic position.

# FLICKER

The wings of flickers catch the eye like flickering light as they fly, and they hammer on trees like carpenters. Either of these characteristics could be the origin of their common name. The Old Icelandic *flak* meant "hanging loosely," or "fluttering." A flicker's call, usually rendered as "wick-a-wick," might also sound like "flicker-flick." *Flick* or *fleck*, another possibility, meant "a light blow," and the colloquial name for the yellow-shafted flicker is yellow*hammer*, used by the Alabama legislature when it designated the flicker as its state bird. The flicker is not, however, related to the European yellowhammer (*see* Bunting).

Flickers are in the Picidae, or woodpecker family. They climb trees and excavate nesting holes, as do other woodpeckers, but they take much of their food from the ground and are partial to ants. The flicker's tongue, like that of most woodpeckers, seems incredibly long. Actually, the true tongue is small, but it is attached to a very long basihyal, which is stored in hollow bony tubes that curve from the back of the bill, up over the rear of the skull, along the bird's crest, and down the front of its face. The tongue is coated with sticky saliva, so that any insect it touches instantly adheres to it.

The yellow-shafted flicker and the red-shafted flicker are both now *Colaptes auratus,* from the Greek *kolaptes,* "chisel," and the Latin *auratus,* "golden." But for a long time the red-shafted flicker was considered a separate species, *C. cafer.* Johann Friedrich Gmelin, who edited Linnaeus's *Systema naturae,* apparently confused the Bay of Good Hope in British Columbia, where the bird came from,

**♀ The flicker's tongue is coated with sticky saliva, so that any insect it touches instantly adheres to it.**

with the Cape of Good Hope, and believed it was from South Africa. The name *cafer* was derived from "Kaffir," a term once used for South Africans. Now derogatory, it originally meant an unbeliever, or non-Muslim, from the Arabic *Kafir.* His name for the flicker lasted past the nineteenth century, even though the nineteenth-century ornithologist Elliot Coues had said, "I cannot bring myself to call this bird *C. cafer.*" It would be nice to record that the name was changed out of respect to South Africans, but in fact it remained in use until the two flicker species were joined and it was no longer scientifically appropriate.

# FLYCATCHER

Some flycatchers are so alike that giving them separate names seems a (albeit harmless) superfluity. Apparently some flycatchers can tell their own species from others only by the males' song variation: The males happily consort together, but the more discerning females are receptive only to the mating cries of their own kind, thus keeping the species pure. The western Pacific-slope flycatcher, *Empidonax difficilis,* is so called because it is "difficult," if not impossible, to distinguish from several other species. *Empidonax* is from the Greek *empidos,* "of a gnat," and *anax,* "king," or "lord."

These "kings of gnats" are small birds that catch flying insects. They are members of the Tyrranidae, or tyrant flycatcher family, which includes pewees (named for the sound of their cry). Old World flycatchers, or Muscicapidae (from the Latin *musca,* "a fly," and *capio,* "I take") are not related to tyrant flycatchers (*see* Kingbird).

The greater pewee is *Contopus pertinax,* meaning "short-footed and persistent" in Greek. Until recently it was called Coues' flycatcher, after ornithologist Elliot Coues. He was a military doctor, and until his retirement in 1881, he went on birding expeditions (riding his mule) wherever the army took him. His revolutionary *Key to North American Birds* was written to enable "anyone without the slightest knowledge of ornithology to identify any specimen." He tested it on his wife, who, "without knowing a tarsus from a tail," successfully used it to identify a downy woodpecker! As well as describing birds, Coues was able to describe ghosts that visited him, and when he died, in 1899, his obituary stated that he had "promised some of his friends before his death to appear to them after his demise. . . . Now they are waiting." Whether or not his friends were disappointed, his ideas and his bird books did live on.

♫ The western Pacific-slope flycatcher, *Empidonax difficilis,* is so called because it is "difficult" to distinguish from several other species.

# FRIGATEBIRD

Frigatebirds are as swift and graceful as the ships they're named for. An Italian three-masted pirate ship was a *fregata,* a word also meaning "swindle." The French is *frégate,* and in both French and Italian, as well as English, the ship and bird share the same name. Frigatebirds, often called "man-o'-war birds" by sailors, can catch flying fish and jellyfish from the surface of the sea, but they prefer to steal from other birds. In the air, they jab with cruelly hooked beaks until the victim relinquishes its catch, which the frigatebird then grabs.

Although frigatebirds soar magnificently over the sea, they rarely get wet, except by accident. They have poorly developed preen-oil glands, and their feathers aren't waterproof. Their feet are only partly webbed, and their very long wings (spanning up to seven feet) make it hard for them to take off from the water. They can even drown if they become waterlogged. Frigatebirds spend most of their time cruising, at speeds of up to ninety-five miles an hour. The weight of the bird's entire skeleton is less than that of its feathers.

**⚘ Frigatebirds, called "man-o'-war" birds by sailors, prefer to steal food from other birds.**

The five kinds of frigatebirds are all called *Fregata,* and their species names are mostly descriptive of their size or flight. But the Christmas Island frigatebird is *F. andrewsi,* for Dr. Charles Andrews, who wrote a *Monograph of Christmas Island* in 1900, after visiting there twice. Frigatebirds live in tropical waters, near islands, where they breed and roost at night. The Polynesian islanders occasionally trained them to carry messages between islands.

Frigatebirds prefer to nest and roost in trees, clinging to branches with their clawed feet. Sometimes there is a shortage of trees where they live, and as soon as a male frigatebird finds an acceptable nesting place, he guards it. He attracts females to his chosen site by expanding and contracting a large gular sac under his chin. This looks like a festive red balloon inflating and deflating, and the female, wooed by it, brings the male sticks, with which he builds their nest. They have to guard nest, eggs, and young, because frigatebirds attack one another as well as other birds. However, they can behave unexpectedly, sometimes nesting side by side with boobies, apparently quite amicably. But as soon as the boobies are airborne, all neighborliness is forgotten, and the boobies can become prime victims of piracy.

As parents, frigatebirds are exceptionally devoted. Even after the single chick has learned to fly, it can depend on both parents, especially its mother, to feed it, for up to six months. Young frigatebirds chase one another, pluck feathers off the water, toss and catch scraps between themselves. Meanwhile, their mothers stick around, making sure they have nourishing meals, until they have learned the skills they need for a buccaneering life.

# GANNET AND BOOBY

Gannets are large birds, about the size of a goose, and their name comes from the Anglo-Saxon *ganot,* meaning "goose." William Turner, the dean of Wells, wrote in 1544 that "this goose . . . will fight gallantly with lads that are let down in baskets by a rope to carry them away, not without danger of life." The risk to the "lads" was considered worthwhile to get chicks and eggs for food and medicine, and Turner said that the bird's fat was "most valuable for many a disease."

Gannets nest on high cliff ledges above cold northern seas. They were called "Solan geese" until the eighteenth century and are now in the Sulidae family. Some etymologists attribute *sula* to the Old Norse *sulan,* meaning "cleft stick," because their wing tips cross over their backs. Others believe it's from the Gaelic *suil,* "eye," and *gheur,* "sharp," because these birds see marvelously, spotting fish from high above the sea.

Boobies are of the same family as gannets, but prefer tropical seas and mostly nest on the ground. The Sulidae usually raise one chick, which eats partly digested fish from its parents' throats. Gannets and boobies catch fish and squid by diving down into the sea from heights of up to a hundred feet, sometimes hitting the water at sixty miles per hour. They plunge deep down, usually collecting the stunned fish on their way up to the surface. They are protected from the terrific impact with the water by a torpedolike shape and the cushioning air sacs under their skin; they have no nostrils. Their feet are large and completely webbed (totipalmate), and they use them to incubate their eggs.

♉ **A perception of stupidity gave boobies their common name, which comes from the Spanish, *bobo*, "silly."**

The northern gannet once nested in huge colonies on Bass Island in the Firth of Forth, from where it gets its scientific name, *Morus bassanus. Morus* means "silly." This perception of stupidity also gave the boobies their common name, because, in spite of Turner's description of gannets bravely defending their young, sailors found that boobies "stupidly" allowed themselves to be captured without resistance. "Booby" comes from the Spanish *bobo,* "silly," which in turn is from the Latin *balbus,* meaning stammeringly inarticulate (and so seemingly foolish). We still have "booby prizes" for those who don't win.

Boobies perform ritual dance displays when mating, then male and female take turns incubating. When ready to take its place on the nest, the booby dances for its partner. The male blue-footed booby dances exuberantly, lifting his feet high to make sure the female takes note of his flashy color and doesn't confuse him with the red-footed booby (*Sula sula*), which inhabits the same tropical seas.

The blue-footed booby was not named until 1882, when it was called *S. nebouxii,* for Dr. Adolphe Simon Néboux, who in 1839 had brought a specimen back to France from the Pacific, after a thirty-one-month voyage on the ship *La Vénus.* Maybe it was just as well Néboux himself hadn't named this booby. He called another bird *dupetithouarsii,* after his captain, Abel du Petit-Thouars. If he could bestow such a name on a mere pigeon, what might he have called a bird with stunningly brilliant azure feet?

# GOATSUCKER

**G**oatsuckers often stay near livestock, where the insects they eat congregate. It was once thought that at night they also sucked the milk of goats, whereupon, wrote Aristotle, "the udder withers and the goat goes blind." Their family name, Caprimulgidae, comes from the Latin *caper,* "goat," and *mulgere,* "to milk." Their Italian and German names, *succiacapre* and *Ziegenmelker,* have the same meaning. They are called nightjars, too, for their "jarring" nocturnal cries. The *Caprimulgus europaeus* is the only goatsucker found in Europe, but it doesn't stay for the winter.

In 1741 Mark Catesby wrote to John Bartram, the Quaker botanist (and father of William Bartram), "There is a bird in Virginia and Carolina, and I suppose in Pennsylvania, that at night calls Whipper Will, and, sometimes, Whip Will's widow, by which names it is called (as the bird clink-eth, the fool thinketh)." The chuck-will's-widow, *C. carolinensis,* is larger than the whippoorwill, called *C. vociferus* ("noisy"). These two American goatsuckers were given their strange common names from the sounds of their cries.

♫ **It was once thought that at night these birds sucked the milk of goats.**

The common poorwill is *Phalaenoptilus nuttallii, Phalaenoptilus* meaning "moth-feathered," and *nuttallii* for Thomas Nuttall. Nuttall could not procure a specimen of the poorwill he described to John Audubon. This was because, wrote Audubon, "he is not in the habit of carrying a gun on his rambles." In fact, Nuttall did carry a gun, but he most often used it to dig up plants, and once when his party was threatened by Indians it was found blocked with mud.

Nighthawks are also in the Caprimulgidae family. They also catch insects in their wide gaping mouths, which makes them look a bit like frogs. The Creoles called the nighthawk *crapaud volant,* or "flying toad." The nighthawks (which aren't related to hawks), have sharp curved bills but are otherwise much like goatsuckers. They both have weak bills, large eyes, and small feet, and on the ground they can only stagger.

Goatsuckers, with their strange voices and nocturnal habits, have always frightened people. Catesby wrote, "The Indians say these birds were never known [until the English came] and that they are the souls or departed spirits of the massacred Indians." Actually the Indians did have names for goatsuckers, and certainly must have heard their eerie cries in the lonely darkness of night.

# GOLDFINCH

The scientific names of both the American and the Eurasian goldfinches mean "thistle-eating," from the Latin *carduus,* "a thistle." The Eurasian bird is *Carduelis carduelis.* The American one, *C. tristis,* meaning "sad thistle eater," was named by Linnaeus, some say, with reference to its song. But Linnaeus was never in America, where goldfinches are generally considered cheery birds.

The European goldfinch might more properly have been called "sad." The red patches on its cheeks and face were said to be smears of Christ's blood, left when a goldfinch tried to remove the crown of thorns at the crucifixion. "It is the greatest wonder," wrote Konrad von Megenburg, a fifteenth-century naturalist, "that the bird sings so beautifully, although it feeds on the sharp spines of a thistle. . . . Dear God . . . thou art well acquainted with thorny food."

Goldfinches are in the large Fringillidae, or finch, family. In Latin, *fringilla* meant a small bird, and many small seed-eating birds are called finches (*see* Chaffinch). It has, however, been suggested that the name could come from *frigus,* meaning "cold," because (in Europe, anyway) they often thrive, and sing, in cold weather. Both American and European goldfinches were sometimes called "wild canaries" because they were thought, correctly, to be related to canaries. But the American male goldfinch's bright plumage is only seasonal, and he looks more like a sparrow after the breeding season.

♫ The goldfinch, wrote the ornithologist Schuyler Mathews, can "cram so much pure *fun* into one short musical sentence!"

American goldfinches breed very late in the year and are sometimes still molting when other birds are building nests. They line their nests with thistledown, so it is often said that they wait for the thistles to produce seed and down. But goldfinches were in America before thistles, which came with European settlers: "A Scotch minister brought with him a bed stuffed with thistle down [and] . . . ye inhabitants having plenty of feathers soon turned out the down," which germinated and spread to become a "very troublesome weed," observed John Bartram.

The goldfinch, wrote the ornithologist Schuyler Mathews in 1904, can "cram so much pure *fun* into one short musical sentence!" They were kept to sing in cages and were sometimes called "draw" birds, because they could be trained to pull food and water toward them. Audubon described a caged goldfinch "obliged to draw towards its bill a little chariot filled with food." Pulling on the chain and preventing it from rolling back again not only requires coordination but vision. So perhaps it's appropriate that the Christ child was often painted holding or innocently playing with a goldfinch, which presaged the ominous tragedy ahead.

# GOOSE

Those seeking elusive information are said to be going on a "wild-goose chase," derived from a Tudor equestrian game of following a leader wherever he rode. Not a bad parallel, considering the complicated story of our long connection with the goose.

We have eaten geese from time immemorial and have used their feathers to "make into cushions so that the necks of the spoiled may rest more softly," as the Italian historian Platina wrote in 1468. We have also simultaneously revered them. The German goddess Freya was goose-footed, and sacred geese guarding the Temple of Juno in Rome alerted the city that the Gauls were at-tacking. A goose's wishbone was used for divination, and in 1455 Jacob Hartlieb wrote, "Teutonic knights in Prussia waged all their wars by the goose-bone."

**A goose's wishbone was used for divination; in Prussia, knights consulted goose bones before every battle.**

Geese are larger than ducks and smaller than swans, but all are Anseriformes, from the Latin *anser,* "goose." Geese are less fully aquatic than their relatives. Their legs are set farther forward, so that they balance and walk well, and they spend much of their waking hours grazing, consuming masses of vegetation to obtain enough nutritional value. They have no real crop to break down their food and so digest rapidly and inefficiently, excreting almost nonstop.

A group of flying geese is called a "skein," because it looks like a length of thread. Alexander Wilson described geese flying north to unknown regions, "shut out since creation from the prying eye of man." Early naturalists didn't know where the brant and barnacle geese had been when they returned south from their breeding grounds. Some thought they hatched from

logs floating in the sea, and as late as 1613 the poet Michael Drayton wrote of a "soft and sappy gum from which these tree-geese
grow." These growths were called "barnacles," meaning "goose-
bearing shells."

Bishop Alexander Neckham said, in 1187, "Birds which do not
emerge from eggs follow the laws relating to fishes as regards
food" and hence can be eaten on fast days, but Pope Innocent III
disagreed with him, and took barnacle geese off the Lenten
menu. The name of brant geese comes either from the Greek
*brenthos,* "a waterbird," or *brandgas,* "burnt" in Old Norse (these
geese are black).

Since they eat continuously, geese can be enormously fattened if confined, and Pliny the Elder described enlarging their
livers by "cramming." Geese that grazed on cut, harvested fields
to be fattened for Michaelmas Day were called "stubble" geese.
When the Gregorian calendar was introduced to Britain in 1752,
there were riots for the eleven days "stolen" from September,
and complaints that Michaelmas geese could not be fattened in
time for the feast.

"Goose" was *gās* in Old Norse and *ghans* in Indo-European. The
German *gacksen* gave us "ganders" (males), "goslings" (young), and
"gaggles" (groups). "Goose-stepping" describes marching without bending the knees, but actually geese, like other birds, walk
on the end joints of their toes, so that what appear to be their

knees are really their ankles. When approached, geese hiss inef-
fectually and waddle away as fast as they can. Because of this, we
call them "silly." But really they have not gained much from any
close acquaintance with us!

# GRACKLE

The naturalist Peter Kalm, Linnaeus's favorite pupil, was sent by the Swedish government to explore North America. When he saw grackles, he reported that they "bear in many points so great a likeness to the daw, the starling and the thrush it is difficult to determine to which genus they belong."

The bird's common name, grackle, comes from *gracula,* which was Latin for the European jackdaw, a small crow. Mark Catesby, who was also in touch with Linnaeus, called grackles "Purple Jack Daws." Linnaeus gave the grackle the name *Quiscalus quiscula,* probably from the Latin *quis,* "who," and *qualis,* "of what kind?" Some etymologists find this unacceptable and suggest that Linnaeus was referring to the Latin *quiscalis,* "quail," but this seems as unlikely, because he was certainly familiar with quails, to which grackles bear no resemblance. As late as 1871 John Burroughs called them "Crow Blackbirds." Considering the mixed descriptions of grackles, Linnaeus's interrogative name seems quite appropriate. They now seem to be settled as icterids in the Ember-izidae family (*see* Blackbird).

In addition to difficulty classifying them, early Americans had mixed feelings about grackles. Swedish immigrants called them "corn thieves." In spring they flocked after farmers sowing corn in such numbers that, wrote Kalm, "it is surprising how they find room to move their wings." According to Kalm, they were controlled chiefly in two ways. Farmers would either shoot them or soak a bit of corn seed in hellebore juice: "When the corn thief eats a grain or two which are so prepared, his head is made dizzy and he falls down: this frightens his companions, and they dare not venture to the place again."

These controls must have been quite effective, for by 1750 Kalm reported that grackles were "rarely seen" in New England. But, he observed, at about that time "an immense quantity of worms appeared," which "did more mischief now than the birds did before," so "the people repented of their emnity." By the next century grackles were acknowledged to control grubs and cutworms, and John Audubon called the corn they took a "tithe." Grackles still descend on fields, making their way across them in a black rolling wave, the birds at the back flying to the front as the ground is cleared of food. They roost in masses so dense that a

> Swedish immigrants called them "corn thieves" because in spring, they flocked after farmers sowing corn.

tree full of them seems, as described by Alexander Wilson, "as if hung in mourning."

When seen from a distance grackles appear plain black, but close up their color changes as the light reflects off them, through brilliant shimmering blues, greens, purple, and bronze. "No painter however gifted," wrote Audubon, and he must have been including himself, "could ever imitate them."

# GREBE

Grebes are truly water-birds. Their nests are often floating plat-forms anchored to a few reeds, and the chicks swim instantly, riding on their parents' backs when they are tired and staying on even when the parent dives deep underwater.

The grebe's former family name was Colymbidae, given by Linnaeus, but in 1956 (*see* Loon) the grebes were settled in a separate family (of which they are the only members), the Podicipedidae. This is from the Greek *podex,* "rump," and *pes,* "foot," meaning "rump-footed" (sometimes "arse-footed"), because their legs are set extremely far back on their bodies.

Although they are awkward on land, they dive deep and swim extensively under water to catch fish. Their feet aren't totally webbed but are lobed along the toes, closing tightly for minimal water resistance on the recovery swimming stroke. They can sink underwater quickly by compressing their feathers to force out air. Grebes' wings are short, and some species can't fly at all.

Because their feathers are exceptionally soft and fluffy, grebe skins were once used for ladies' muffs and collars. Grebes pluck out their own feathers and eat them, probably as a protection against any sharp fish bones in their digestive tracts. The chicks are fed their parents' downy feathers before getting any other food.

*Grebe* (French name, *grèbe*) is probably from the Breton word *krib,* or "crest," describing the crested head plumes of many grebes, especially during the breeding season. The elaborate courtship rituals of the great crested grebe take place in water, as do most aspects of their lives. When mating, these grebes dive, weave, offer each other bouquets of water plants, and patter rapidly along the surface of the water. Sometimes these passionately erotic dances take place by moonlight, with the culminative union not in the water but more likely on a floating bed of weeds.

**When mating, great crested grebes dive, weave, and offer each other bouquets of water plants; sometimes these passionately erotic dances take place by moonlight.**

# GROUSE

Grouse are in the order Galliformes, from the Latin for "chickenlike," and they spend much of their time scratching for food on the ground, where they also nest. Like domestic chickens, they continue to lay eggs (even if some are removed) until a large clutch is ready for hatching. The chicks are hatched ready to run around. They develop completely inside the eggs, which consequently have large rich yolks. The chicks have high peeping calls, keeping them in contact with their parents and one another. The grouse is closely related to the ptarmigan and the prairie chicken. All have feather-covered nostrils and legs and can be found in northern parts of the world.

When courting, the male American ruffed grouse perches on a large log and beats his wings rapidly until the pressure of air forced down produces a hollow booming sound. This grouse, *Bonasa umbellus* (*Bonasa* means "bison"), was so named by Linnaeus because the courting sounds like the drumming of many hooves.

*Umbella* means "a parasol," which is what his tail looks like when spread. Grouse are polygamous, and the male contributes nothing but his genes to the family, which is raised by the female. This explains his preoccupation with mating rituals, which are his only family responsibilities.

**🦅 The ptarmigan's name comes from the Gaelic *tarmachan,* meaning "a croaker," describing the bird's hoarse croaking cry.**

The male ptarmigan *does* help his mate raise their family. This bird is called *Lagopus* because of its very feathery legs, which appear furry like those of a hare (from the Greek *lagos,* "a hare," and *pous,* "a foot"). This extra insulation is needed for warmth in the grouse's cold northern homeland. It molts three times yearly to blend in with the changing seasons, and it sometimes sleeps under the snow, diving headfirst into it. The common name ptarmigan comes from the Gaelic *tarmachan,* meaning "a croaker," describing the bird's hoarse croaking cry, heard on the Highland moors. In 1684 a professor of medicine in Edinburgh, Robert Sibbald, describing the ptarmigan in *Scotia Illustrator,* added a "p" to the name, believing that it came from a Greek word.

Although the American prairie chicken ("heath hen") of the northeast is now extinct, the greater and the lesser prairie chicken exist further south. Their generic name, *Tympanuchus,* comes from the Greek *tympanon,* "a drum." These birds use their throats, not their wings, to make their courtship drumming noise. On each side of their neck is a vivid orange sac the size of a plum, which they blow up and deflate to make a booming sound. The greater prairie chicken, *T. cupido,* was named by Linnaeus, probably for the tufts of feathers on the neck, reminiscent of little Cupid's wings.

Settlers in America were delighted to find grouse, familiar from Europe, where they were called "grows" or "grewes." Until recently Americans commonly called them "fool hens" because, intent on the delights of courtship, they were often slow to recognize the epicurean intentions of humans.

# GULL

You've got to understand that a seagull is an unlimited idea of freedom," wrote Richard Bach in his concentratedly uplifting and ornithologically unreliable *Jonathan Livingston Seagull* (1970). "Seagulls" often reflect dreams of open seas, but actually there is no bird of that name, and gulls are often found inland. In spite of Jonathan Livingston's desire for improvement, gulls are already among the world's most successful birds and fly magnificently. They have adapted to different conditions worldwide, and the swallow-tailed gull of the Galápagos Islands can even see at night.

The name "gull" is from the medieval Cornish *gullan,* or *gwylan,* "throat," which comes from the Celtic *wylo,* "wail." Gulls were usually called "mews" (for their cry) until the fifteenth century. *Gullan* was probably shortened to "gull" because it was thought to be plural (like oxen).

By Shakespeare's time a "gull" also meant someone who was "gullible." Gullible people swallow anything, including lies, and gulls eat anything, even one another's stray chicks. Or a "gull," once any easily caught young seabird, might thus be "gullible."

Omnivorous herring gulls expertly drop shellfish onto hard surfaces to break them. Fishermen used to watch these gulls to find congregating fish, but nowadays they would probably discover floating garbage, a staple of the gulls' diet.

The family name, Laridae, comes from the Greek *laros,* "seabird." Larids include terns and noddies. Small, graceful terns dive to catch fish, and were called "sea swallows" until their Swedish name, *tarna,* was adopted in the eighteenth century. "Noddy," or fool, was used by sailors be-

> **Gullible people swallow anything, including lies, and gulls eat anything, even one another's stray chicks.**

cause this bird was unafraid of them, and the brown noddy's scientific name, *Anous stolidus,* means "stupid fool." The noddy is a reverse image of a tern: it is dark with a white cap, rather than light with a dark cap, and it has a wedge-shaped, rather than forked, tail.

Gulls often make inland excursions. Bonaparte's gull (named for Napoleon's nephew) nests in trees. A famous trip to dry land occurred in 1848 when Mormon crops were devastated by hordes of grasshoppers, but were miraculously saved by California gulls (which nest on the Great Salt Lake). These gulls ate the grasshoppers and were rewarded with a monument (two gulls on a large ball) in Salt Lake City.

Gulls are mostly white, with gray or black markings. They are murderously rapacious, and their harsh cries are far from the songs of angels. But when their pure plumage tufts the breaking waves and their cries soar up into misty skies, it is no wonder that we dream still of being as free as a "seagull."

# HAWK

**H**awks have strong wings and remarkable eyesight. Spotting their prey from afar, they can seize it at ground level and, "with one fell swoop," wrote Shakespeare in *Macbeth,* kill it with their claws.

Hawks are in the Accipitridae family, from the Latin *accipere,* meaning "to seize." Their common name, hawk, is from the Middle English *hauk* and the Anglo-Saxon *hafoc,* meaning "having." Harrier hawks fly in circles before targeting their victims and often have the prefix *Circus* to their name. They also have round, circular faces. "To harry" is to lay waste or plunder.

Hawks, usually the females, were popular hunting birds, used to take hares or ground birds. These savage birds could be subdued so that, as one old training manual said, "The onely maine poynt, is to have his hawke in love" with her owner. But by the time Europeans settled in America, hunting with birds had been replaced by guns, and farmers hunted hawks because they killed chickens and game birds. John Audubon described a farmer felling an oak to destroy the nest of a red-tailed hawk: "the poor mother-bird sails sorrowfully over and around. . . . The noble tree crashes to the earth . . . The work of revenge has been accomplished."

**A "haggard hawk" was an untamed female hawk more than two years old.**

Audubon tried, unsuccessfully, to rename the Cooper's hawk for Lord Stanley. This English aristocrat from Liverpool, Audubon excitedly told his wife, Lucy, got "down on his knees, looking at my work." Perhaps it was more for practicality than reverence, though, because many of the life-sized drawings were too large for an ordinary table! Earlier, in Philadelphia, Audubon had written that Edward Harris "looked at the drawings I had for sale and said he would take them *all,* at my prices. I would have kissed him, but that is not the custom in this icy city." He gratefully named the Harris's hawk for his patron.

Audubon also knew William Swainson, whose name was given to *Buteo swainsoni* (*buteo* is Latin for "hawk" or "buzzard"). After visiting the Swainsons in London he wrote home, "Such talks on birds we have had together. Why, Lucy, thou would'st think that birds were all we cared for in this world, but thou knowest this is not so." He was no doubt trying to reassure Lucy, who had endured plenty for his preoccupation with birds.

Audubon often left his family for prolonged periods to promote his work, and for a while Lucy supported herself and their two sons by teaching. Another trial for Lucy was that women often fell for Audubon. Once in New Orleans he was followed by an anonymous veiled lady, later revealed to be exquisitely beautiful. She asked him to paint her in the nude, and paid him with a gun engraved with his name, which he greatly treasured.

Hawks were caught and trained for hunting at various ages. A "haggard hawk" was an untamed female hawk more than two years old. Originally "haggard" meant "living in a hedge" (from the Old German *hag,* "a hedge"), and then it came to mean "wild." A haggard person, however, is worn and disheveled, rather than wildly free like a young hawk—even though the word has the same root.

# HERON

Herons look like prehistoric ghosts, and indeed they are among our most ancient birds. Our ancestors, who revered them, noticed how high up they fly: "where," wrote Rabanus Maurus in the ninth century, "they behold forever, the countenance of God." Large flying herons can be recognized by their curved, retracted necks hunched back between their shoulders. Their wings are deeply cambered, allowing them to brake and land slowly, and avoid damaging their long delicate legs.

The name "heron" probably derives from the Old English *hragra,* imitative of their harsh cry. Until the seventeenth century they were often called "heronshaw" or "henshaw." In 1635 a Cambridge professor wrote that "the heron or *hernsaw* is a large fowle that . . . hath a marvellous hatred to the hawk, which hatred is duly returned." When Shakespeare's Hamlet was apparently losing his mind he said he could still distinguish "a hawk from a handsaw," meaning a heron. Heron-hawking was a popular sport, still being practiced in 1861 by the members of the "Royal Loo Hawking Club" in Holland. When caught, herons were considered a table delicacy.

None of the members of the heron family, or Ardeidae (from the Latin *ardea,* "heron"), has a preen gland, from which most birds obtain oil to condition their feathers. Instead herons have "pulvi- plumes," feathers that disintegrate at the tip, becoming a cleansing powder, which the bird spreads with the comblike edge of its middle toe. Most Ardeidae feed on water creatures, although they also eat small land creatures. The Japanese green- backed heron *Butorides striatus* ("like a bittern and striped") has even learned to wait for humans to toss scraps of bread, which it doesn't eat. Instead it drops the bread into the water to bait fish. Other herons use feathers for the same purpose. Some herons dig out mud dwellers by stirring the silt with their feet, or shake their feet to attract inquisitive fish.

> Our ancestors revered herons and noticed how high up they fly, "where they behold forever, the countenance of God," wrote Rabanus Maurus.

Herons often nest in colonies. They have elaborate courtship rituals and are more leisurely about mating than some birds, spending up to fifteen seconds on copulation. (A sparrow only gives it one second!) Afterward they may shake and preen, cross necks, and exchange sticks. Then the parents, which look alike, proceed to share the child-rearing duties.

# HOATZIN

**W**ithout traveling, not many of us can hope to see a South American hoatzin. This bird is in some ways more similar to distant prehistoric birds than to other birds today. Unlike other modern birds, baby hoatzins are able to crawl like quadrupeds, using hooked claws on their wings. In just this way, it is thought, the ancient *archaeopteryx* ("ancient wing") moved slowly from land to trees. When disturbed or frightened, baby hoatzins jump down from their nest overhanging water, swim ashore, and slowly climb back when the danger is past. As their feathers grow they lose their claws, thus seeming to pass through an avian evolutionary process in a few weeks.

Hoatzins are the only members of their family, the Opisthocomidae. This, from the Greek *opisthen,* "behind," and *kome,* "hair," refers to their shaggy neck and head plumage.

The word "hoatzin" comes from a Nahuatl Indian name, *uatzin,* and is probably onomatopoeic, based on their hoarse cries and hisses. A Spanish name for the hoatzin is *cigana,* meaning "gypsy," for the bird's bright red eyes colorfully surrounded with a blue patch and its yellow and black crest. They live in mangrove swamps and, more like ruminants than birds, eat leaves, which slowly ferment in their huge crops. Perhaps because of this, hoatzins stink. A full crop makes hoatzins top-heavy, so to balance, they prop themselves against the branches while they eat and digest. All birds are extraordinary, but the hoatzin adds a few strange twists to the miracle of evolution.

A Spanish name for them is *cigana,* meaning "gypsy," for the bird's bright red eyes colorfully surrounded with a blue patch and its yellow and black crest.

# HUMMINGBIRD

Hummingbirds, in the Trochilidae family, were named by Linnaeus for the *trokhilos,* or "crocodile bird," which, according to Herodotus, hopped inside the crocodile's mouth to eat leeches. But, Herodotus wrote, "the crocodile likes this, so never hurts the bird." They *are* small and agile, but hummingbirds are New World birds, never found in the Old World, in or out of crocodiles' jaws.

The ruby-throated hummingbird is the only hummingbird that breeds in the northeastern United States, where early settlers marveled at it. To one early naturalist, the bird's flight sounded "like a humble bee . . . wherefore she is called Humbird." In 1854 Ludwig Reichenbach, the director of the Zoological Museum at Dresden, named the ruby-throated *Archilochus colubris,* after Archilochus, a minor Greek poet who, unlike most Greeks, admitted that he was a coward who had run away in battle. Reichenbach must have been thinking of the hummingbird's unique ability to fly in any direction, including backward, like Archilochus. *Colibris* is probably a South American name.

Ruby-throated hummingbirds migrate from South America to southern Canada and are anything but cowardly. They are unafraid of humans, and battle furiously between themselves. To cross the Gulf of Mexico they fly nonstop for five hundred miles. Any adverse conditions mean certain death, and one marvels that they dare to attempt the journey at all.

> ♫ To one early naturalist the bird's flight sounded "like a humble bee . . . wherefore she is called Humbird."

The smallest bird in the world is the bee hummingbird, *Mellisuga helenae,* from the Latin, *mel,* "honey," and *sugo,* "I suck." Hummingbirds live mostly on nectar that they suck from flowers. The bird was most likely named by the German ornithologist John Gundlach; Helen was the wife of a Cuban coffee planter, Charles Booth, whom Gundlach visited in 1839. Gundlach lived in Cuba for over fifty years.

Early explorers to the New World were astonished by the hummingbirds' brilliant iridescent color and the way they use their wings like rotating propellers to hover in midair. They are in the same order as swifts, the Apodiformes, meaning "without feet" (*see* Swift). Hummingbirds can't walk or hop, but they do perch, and they do have feet. Their preferred flowers are often red (a color insects can't see) and without scent or landing platforms. These flowers apparently evolved to attract hummingbirds, more reliable pollinators than insects (which don't fly in bad weather). Certain flower mites even depend on hummingbirds to travel from flower to flower; they leap onto the bird's bill while it feeds, ride to the next flower, then rapidly disembark before the bird leaves again. Hummingbirds have the highest metabolism of almost any warm-blooded creature and they feed constantly, sometimes becoming torpid at night to conserve energy.

Brazilian explorers called hummingbirds *beija flor,* or "kiss flower." And the Mayans, who found them captivating, believed that hummingbirds were made from bright scraps left over from the creation of other birds.

# IBIS

In ancient Egypt killing an ibis, "whether intentionally or not," was, according to the Greek historian Herodotus, punishable by death. Thoth, the Egyptian god of wisdom and learning, had the body of a man and the head of an ibis. The Egyptians mummified both the birds and their eggs, and their family name, Threskiornithidae, is Greek for "sacred bird." *Ibis* was the bird's Egyptian name, used by the Greeks as well.

Ibises were revered because they caught and ate dangerous "flying snakes," wrote Herodotus. In fact, ibises eat mostly crustaceans and insects, which they find in or near water. They are wading birds, with unwebbed feet and long curved bills, and they have bare or partly bare heads and necks. The southern bald ibis is *Geronticus calvus,* meaning "a bald-headed old man."

Ibises mostly grunt or hiss. The sixteenth-century Swiss naturalist Konrad Gesner named the waldrapp ibis (or northern bald ibis) from the German *Wald,* "wood," and *Rapp,* "raven," because of its ravenlike croak. It was hunted for food, and by the late eighteenth century, this ibis had died out in Europe and no known ibis fitted Gesner's description. Waldrapp ibises were later seen in Egypt, and their name is *G. eremita,* meaning "an old hermit."

In the New World ibises were hunted until quite recently both for food and feathers. The beautiful red feathers of the scarlet ibis were particularly in demand for artificial flowers. Early American naturalists confused ibises with herons, storks, and curlews, and they were first given the name *Tantalus* (*see* Limpkin). The only native American stork is still sometimes called a "wood ibis" (*see* Stork).

**♀ Egyptians mummified both the birds and their eggs.**

John Audubon described seeing the white ibis and its young, and he didn't hesitate to inform his readers of "the pain of the numerous scratches and lacerations of my legs," which he received on the grueling search. The New World white and scarlet ibises are called *Eudocimus albus* ("white") and *E. ruber* ("red"), respectively. *Eudocimus* comes from the Greek *eu,* "well," and *dokimus,* "tried," and was given to them by Johann Wagler, a nineteenth-century ornithologist from Munich. "Well-tried" was Wagler's way of demonstrating his satisfaction at finally classifying these two American birds. Wagler loved nomen-clature and once described sorting bird names as a way of "pass-ing the hours in the most pleasant manner imaginable."

# JAY

About the time automobiles became common, and dangerous, a "jaywalker" meant a rustic bumpkin who didn't look where he was going. And a "jay" has often meant a silly person. In fact, like all corvids, jays are very intelligent. Maybe their reputation for foolishness came from their vociferous chatter, or perhaps because they were supposedly vain about their gaudy plumage.

The harsh metallic call of a jay is not unlike the sound of screaming brakes (when slammed on to avoid jaywalkers?). Even so, Mark Catesby thought that the newly discovered American blue jay was "more tuneful" than its Eurasian namesake. The noisy ("garrulous") Eurasian jay, *Garrulus glandarius,* is more reddish grey than blue, although it has brilliant blue bars on its wings. *Glandarius* is from *glans,* Latin for "acorn," which all jays relish and often bury for future use. By forgetting where they have stored acorns, "these birds alone are capable in a few years' time to replant all the cleared lands," wrote William Bartram.

The English name "jay" comes from the Old French *jai* and was probably first used in Britain after the Norman invasion. The name more likely came from its "gay" (brightly colored) plumage than (as is sometimes suggested) the Roman name *Gaius*. A twelfth-century book entitled *Beast Fables* popularized a practice of giving human names to wild creatures.

The blue jay, *Cyanocitta cristata* (from the Greek *kyanos*, "blue," and *kitta*, "jay"), is the very first bird in Alexander Wilson's famous nineteenth-century *American Ornithology*, and he surmised, correctly, that this "beau among the feathered tenants of our woods" is uniquely American. Farther north, the Canadian, or gray, jay *(Perisoreus canadensis)* was notorious for stealing from trappers and explorers.

⚲ **About the time automobiles became common, a "jaywalker" was a rustic bumpkin who didn't look where he was going.**

They had to watch out for it constantly, and complained that it took everything, from candles, pens, and soap to the bait in their traps. They called it "Whiskey Jack," a name that reflects its roguish role but may come from the Algonquin name *Wis-ka-tjan*. *Perisoreus*, from the Greek *perisoreuo*, "to heap up," referring to the bird's habit of caching its own food (as well as stolen camp supplies).

Steller's jay, *C. stelleri*, is called after Georg Wilhelm Steller, a German naturalist who took part in an expedition sponsored by the Russian empress Catherine the Great and led by the famous commander Vitus Bering. When he first saw this jay in the unknown territory of Alaska, Steller said, "This bird proved to me we were really in America." In the winter of 1741 Bering's ship, the *St. Peter,* was wrecked on what is now Bering Island, where the commander died. The crew survived the freezing conditions, living in pits covered with sailcloth. Steller didn't lose his enthusiasm as a naturalist, and he spent his free time writing about birds and animals. He managed to persuade his reluctant companions to dissect a huge beached manatee, while Arctic foxes hungrily surrounded the men as they worked. Steller's name was given to two other birds and a sea lion, as well as his jay. But most deservedly was the manatee, so laboriously dissected, named Steller's sea cow.

# KESTREL

Although it's not a hawk, Americans often still call the American kestrel a "sparrowhawk." Its name *Falco sparverius* means "sparrow falcon," because this small falcon was thought to eat sparrows. The European sparrowhawk isn't a falcon, but an accipter (*see* Hawk).

In fact, kestrels eat fewer sparrows than insects and mice. Cones in their eyes that can detect ultraviolet light help them catch voles. They can perceive the iridescent reflection of the urine squirted by the rodents to mark their trails. Kestrels have the long pointed wings, brown eyes, and notched upper bill of other falcons. Their common name refers to their harsh call, deriving from the Latin *crepitare,* "to rattle," which in Middle English became *kastil,* and in French *crécelle.* The European kestrel, *F. tinnunculus,* gets its name from the Latin *tinnio,* "I ring." They were traditionally kept near dovecotes because, as a sixteenth-century writer put it, "they fear away other haukes with their ringing voice."

The male kestrel brings prey whole to the nest, and the female breaks up anything that is too big for the chicks to swallow. If the female dies, the male will sometimes continue to feed the chicks, but he lacks the instinct to prepare their food and may deposit hearty meals beside his young as they starve to death.

♪ **Their common name refers to their harsh call.**

# KINGBIRD

The life of the eastern kingbird "is one continual scene of broils and battles," wrote Alexander Wilson in his *American Ornithology*. At that time the bird's scientific name, given by the French naturalist Louis Vieillot, was *Tyrannus intrepidus* ("intrepid tyrant"). Now it is *Tyrannus tyrannus,* meaning a tyrant twice over. The kingbird's reputation for ferocity, especially during the breeding season, has not diminished, and in 1935 an ornithologist reported seeing one attack a low-flying airplane!

The flycatcher family, Tyrannidae, is the largest family of New World birds (*see* Flycatcher). The kingbird does pursue flying insects but also eats fruit and grubs. It was once called the bee martin (*see* Swallow) because of its supposed fondness for eating bees. Beekeepers hunted it mercilessly.

*T. vociferans* is called Cassin's kingbird, for John Cassin, curator of ornithology at the Academy of Natural Sciences in Philadelphia in the mid-eighteen hundreds. He was interested in foreign as well as American birds, and his imports of specimens from Australia, India, and Africa made the academy's bird collection the largest in the world at that time. Cassin, who was hampered by attacks of arsenic poisoning from his work preparing bird skins, died in 1869, at age fifty-six. Several other birds are named for him.

*An ornithologist reported seeing a kingbird attack a low-flying airplane.*

*T. couchii* was named for General Darius Couch, who in 1853, before serving in the American Civil War, had made a zoological expedition to Mexico and become a proficient birder. Once after he shot a bird, its mate's cry of "exquisite sadness" so moved him that he "felt almost resolved to desist from making further collections in natural history." Couch was not the only ornithologist who expressed regret at shooting a bird in order to identify it.

Kingbirds migrate south in winter, coming north in late spring to breed with aggressive devotion. "He fights for his mate," wrote Mabel Osgood Wright in her 1895 book *Birdcraft,* "he fights to protect his nest, and when he cannot find an opponent he emulates Don Quixote." Around nesting kingbirds enthusiastic bird-watchers might want to avoid waving their arms.

# KINGFISHER

The first bird that John Audubon felt he had successfully depicted was a kingfisher. He had been trying to make the dead birds he drew look alive but, he complained, "Alas they were *dead* . . . neither wing, nor leg, nor tail could I place according to my wishes." Then, while struggling to arrange the corpse of a kingfisher, he had a sudden inspiration. At earliest dawn the next day, he rode into Norristown, Pennsylvania, waited until the store opened, and bought wire and pins. He rode home before breakfast and positioned the carcass realistically, pinning it as if in flight. "I really believe my tenant's wife [landlady] thought I was mad," he wrote, but the new drawing of the kingfisher set the pattern for his subsequent bird portraits, which, to this day, seem to move upon the pages of *Birds of America*.

Audubon's kingfisher was the belted kingfisher, widespread in North America. Its plumage is bluish gray and white (the female has a rusty belly band), rather than the brilliant metallic turquoise blue and orange of the Eurasian kingfisher. American kingfishers are larger than European kingfishers, although their habits are similar. In Britain kingfishers were simply called "fishers" until about 1000 A.D. Then they became "kingsfisschers," perhaps because they caught fish so well, or perhaps because of their shimmering plumage, like the precious metals worn by kings.

> ✎ They were "kingsfisschers," perhaps because they caught fish so well or perhaps because their shimmering plumage was like the precious metals worn by kings.

The Eurasian common kingfisher is *Alcedo atthis,* and the American belted kingfisher is *Megaceryle alcyon. Ceryle* means "seabird" (*mega* is "large"), and *atthis* means "Athenian." *Alcedo* and *alcyon* refer to the Greek goddess Alcyone (or Halcyone) from the Greek *hals,* "sea," and *kuo,* "conceive." Kingfishers were once called halcyons, especially in poetic literature.

Alcyone was the daughter of Aeolus, the god of the wind, and the widow of Ceyx, who drowned at sea. Alcyone threw herself into the sea, on top of her husband's floating body. But as she kissed him and "thrust her growing beak between his lips," wrote Ovid, they were both turned into kingfishers. In spite of this briny story, kingfishers aren't seabirds. Because their unwebbed feet have small stubby toes, they can't really swim but propel themselves in the water with their short wings.

The laughing kookaburra, *Dacelo novaeguinae,* of Australia and Papua New Guinea is a kingfisher, but *it* doesn't even live near streams, and it eats snakes and lizards, not fish. *Dacelo* is simply an anagram of *alcedo,* contrived by ornithologists. Kookaburra is an Aboriginal name imitative of its cry. It is often called a laughing jackass, also because of its harsh cry, typical of kingfishers.

All kingfishers nest in holes—sometimes in trees, sometimes burrowed into banks. A more lyrical ancient belief, however, was that the halcyon built a nest of bones and shells, floating on the open sea. It was specially protected from the waves by the bird's original father, Aeolus, who controlled the wind. He calmed the sea for seven days before and after the winter solstice, while the kingfishers raised their young. This period of quiet, or "halcyon days," was described by John Milton as a breathless time of expectancy before the birth of Christ, when "birds of calm sit brooding on the charmed wave."

# KITE

Children scampering on windswept hills tug toy kites named after this predatory bird. The name "kite" goes far back, and we first find it in the Anglo-Saxon *cyta,* from *skut,* meaning to "swoop" or "shoot." But mostly kites soar, looking for carrion. In *Julius Caesar* Shakespeare describes how they "Fly o'er our head, and downward look on us, / As we were sickly prey."

In the West the first known reference to man-made kites is from the sixteenth century, but they were made in China before the fourth century B.C. Chinese lords experimented by manning kites with surplus prisoners to see if they could fly. They couldn't. But the study of soaring birds was an essential step in the history of air transportation, and it took a while before we realized that people would never fly by flapping wings — we just aren't built right.

The Tudor writer William Turner said that kites were "wont to snatch food out of children's hands." They also, in the days before clothespins, grabbed what Shakespeare calls "lesser linen" left to dry, which they used for nesting material.

Kites are in the Accipitridae, or hawk, family. Many of their names, such as the Greek *Gampsonyx* ("curved claw") and the Latin *Rostrhamus* ("hooked beak") are descriptive. The swallow-tailed kite, *Elanoides forficatus,* is named from *elanos* ("kite") and the Latin word *forficatus,* "scissors." This describes the bird's forked tail and, incidentally, tells us that the Romans used pivoted scissors, just as we do.

*♃ The study of soaring birds was an essential step in the history of air transportation.*

The snail kite, *Rostrhamus sociabilis,* gets its name from its habit of nesting sociably in colonies. Its common name comes from its diet of freshwater apple snails. Unlike most water snails, the apple snails have lungs and must come to the water surface to breathe, where the kites, which can't dive, snatch them up. To eat the snail, they generally wait until it emerges from its shell. Sadly, as humans have encroached on the Florida Everglades, both the snails and the birds, which depend on them for food, have become endangered. It would have been better for these kites if, like their cousins in London, they had developed a taste for children's sandwiches.

# KITTIWAKE

Kittiwakes were described by the mid-twentieth-century Dutch naturalist Niko Tinbergen as "a rather aberrant species of gull." Unlike most gulls, kittiwakes dive five or six feet underwater to catch fish, using their long, thin wings as fins.

And unlike other gulls, the female kittiwake *sits* to copulate, presumably to avoid falling off the high, narrow ledge where the birds both mate and nest. The pair waits to build a nest until after rainfall, when mud is available to construct a solid structure that can hold their two eggs (only one of which usually hatches) securely. Kittiwakes don't need to recognize their chick, for it doesn't stray from the precarious nest at all. It learns to fly by facing the cliff wall and flapping its wings.

Because the kittiwake chick has no space to maneuver, it feeds directly out of the throats of its parents, who have plain yellow bills. They do not have a bright spot on their lower bill, which the chicks of some gulls peck, stimulating the parents to regurgitate food. Silvery white kittiwake chicks, high on inaccessible ledges, have no need, either, for the brown camouflage typical of baby gulls.

Their common name, kittiwake, comes from their cry and probably originated in Scotland, where it was sometimes spelled "cattiwake." The widespread black-legged kittiwake is *Rissa tridactyla* (Greek for "three-toed"). The red-legged kittiwake, *R. brevirostris* (Latin for "short-beaked"), breeds only on islands in the Bering Sea. *Rissa* is an Icelandic name.

Much of what we know about kittiwakes and other larids was discovered by Niko Tinbergen, the author of the 1953 book *The Herring Gull's World*. He believed in fieldwork, however challenging the conditions. He and his team studied gulls in the chilly

**"Bird watching of this kind just means sitting still."**

Farne Islands, where "observing the birds on the cliff was cold work . . . for bird watching of this kind just means sitting still." One of his gull-watching colleagues "wriggled into a sleeping bag, balancing precariously on the edge of the cliff, and then managed to squeeze in a hot-water bottle." Another hatched gulls' eggs in a cardboard box, which she took into her sleeping bag for the night. "Next morning, after a none too comfortable night, she could proudly produce a box of chicks." The team could then study innate behavior of gulls—and *we* can sit comfortably in our chairs and read all about it!

# KIWI

Kiwis are only found in New Zealand, and "kiwi" is their Maori name. It is said to be imitative of their cry, although these birds include in their vocal repertoire whistles, grunts, mews, growls, and hisses.

Kiwis no longer have living relatives. Their nearest relation was the moa, which was hunted to extinction by New Zealanders before (for once!) European explorers arrived. They are the smallest of the ratites, none of which can fly (*see* Ostrich), and in some ways are more evocative of little animals than birds, with shaggy feathers more like coarse fur. They live in burrows, eating mostly earthworms. Their short, bare legs are stout, and they can run fast. Unlike any other bird, their nostrils are at the *tip* of their long bill, and they hunt by smell, mostly at night, poking in the ground for grubs and worms, then clearing dirt from their nostrils by blowing and grunting.

The kiwi's name, *Apteryx,* is from the Greek *a,* "without," and *pteron,* "feathers" or "wings," which refers to their tiny unfeathered wings. They have no tails. There are three species of kiwis. The brown kiwi's name, *Apteryx australis,* doesn't mean "Australian" (there aren't any kiwis in Australia) but "southern," for the bird comes from South Island, New Zealand. *A. owenii* is called after Sir Richard Owen, known for his vigorous opposition to Charles Darwin. Owen tried to prove that certain human brain lobes were missing in apes, so they couldn't possibly be related to humans. The British magazine *Punch* published this verse about Owen's and Darwin's controversy: " 'Tis brain versus brain, / 'Til one of them's slain, / By Jove! It will be a good match!"

**Kiwifruit is the same compact shape as the bird, as well as being brown and furry—and definitely unable to fly.**

Kiwis themselves are odd enough to challenge evolutionary preconceptions about birds. Few people ever even see a kiwi, which leaves its burrow at night, tapping the ground with its bill like a blind person. The male incubates their one huge egg, larger in proportion to the kiwi's body than the egg of any other bird, weighing about a quarter of the female's weight. This might be the equivalent of a human mother giving birth to a thirty-pound baby—so it's understandable that the female kiwi leaves the rest of the parenting to the male.

New Zealanders have taken this curious bird as their national emblem. Sometimes they even call themselves "Kiwis," an epithet particularly used for nonflying members of their air force. The kiwifruit is not eaten by kiwi birds. It was known as the Chinese gooseberry until it was introduced to New Zealand in 1904 and developed commercially there. The nickname helped popularize the fruit, which is the same compact shape as the bird, as well as being brown and furry—and definitely unable to fly.

# LARK

Perhaps the most heartrending ornithological argument in all of literature is that of Juliet trying to persuade Romeo that the bird they hear is "the nightingale, and not the lark, / That pierc'd the fearful hollow of thine ear." Romeo sadly insists, "It was the lark, the herald of the morn." If the bird is a lark, dawn has come, and the doomed lovers know they must separate.

The English name "lark" seems to come from *lawerce,* originally Anglo-Saxon for "traitor." No connection of the lark with treachery has been unraveled, but the name may be associated with ancient beliefs connected to sunrise. Everybody agrees that early risers get up "with the lark," and some people even suggest this could be when lovers "lark around," or frolic, before anyone else is awake to see them.

These birds were simply called larks, or (in Scotland) lavrocks, until the seventeenth century, when the name skylark was first used. It is thought to be a translation of the earlier Swiss naturalist Konrad Gesner's German name for the bird,

*Himmellerch*. The skylark flutters high into the sky while singing. Its name *Alauda arvensis* is from *alauda,* meaning "lark" in Latin, and *arvus,* "a field." Skylarks inhabit open spaces, building nests in shallow grassy depressions. Their drab plumage blends with the ground.

**♫ A group of larks is poetically called an "exaltation."**

European emigrants sometimes tried to take skylarks with them, successfully introducing them to Australia and Canada. They can still be found in Vancouver Island, Washington state, and Hawaii. Unlike many birds, skylarks flourish in cultivated open areas, so although they were brought to Long Island in the nineteenth century, they died out as fields there diminished.

The only true lark native to North America is the horned lark, *Eremophila alpestris;* the name means "loving mountain solitude." It has a lark's typical long back toe and feeds on the ground, walking rather than hopping. It also sings in flight high above the ground. The crested lark, *Galerida cristata* (from the Latin *galerum,* "helmetlike"), is widespread in Asia, Africa, and Europe (but not Britain). *G. theklae* was touchingly named after Christian Ludwig Brehm's daughter Thekla who died at the age of twenty-six. In 1822, Brehm published a book on "many rare or insufficiently observed German birds" (*see* Nuthatch).

The meadowlark of North America is the state bird of Kansas, Montana, Nebraska, North Dakota, Oregon, and Wyoming. Although they sing exuberantly and nest on open ground, meadowlarks are not really larks. They are bigger than larks, with breasts of "a fair yellow colour," as Mark Catesby wrote. Meadowlarks are icterids, like New World blackbirds (*see* Blackbird), but with etymological imprecision are named *Sturnella,* which means "little starling." Starlings aren't larks *or* blackbirds!

The two American meadowlarks—the eastern meadowlark, *Sturnella magna* ("large"), and the western meadowlark—are so similar that even the females can only distinguish their own species by the sound of the male's song. John Audubon was the first ornithologist to differentiate between them. He called the western meadowlark *S. neglecta,* because he thought it had been neglected by earlier, less observant ornithologists.

A group of larks is poetically called an "exaltation." Shelley said the skylark's rhapsodic song could not be of this world at all, and that the lark was not a bird but a "blithe Spirit!" Even those of us who have never heard a real lark singing know exactly what to "sing like a lark" means.

# Limpkin

The limpkin's cry has a quality of unutterable sadness, as though the bird is wailing in despair at the desolation of its watery surroundings. Florida Indians called it the "crying bird." William Bartram, traveling to Florida in 1776, called it *Tantalus,* after the criminal king of Lydia who served the gods a stew of his own son and was punished by having to stand for eternity in waist-deep water, with succulent fruit just out of reach above and water receding whenever he bent to drink.

Like King Tantalus, limpkins often stand in water, searching for their favorite food, the large, greenish apple snail, but they also eat other water and land creatures. They bend down underwater to take the snails and, with an asymmetrical bill, curved conveniently to the right to match the shell's contours, they neatly extricate the occupant, leaving the shells in heaps where they feed. Ornithologists watching limpkins feed say they sometimes hold their prey for a bit, as if pausing to reflect before enjoying a good meal. Their common name "limpkin" refers to the way they walk, seeming to favor one leg.

> **The name "limpkin" refers to the way they walk, seeming to favor one leg.**

Limpkins, no longer called after the suffering king, are now the only members of the Aramidae family. *Aramos* is the Greek for a kind of heron. Once *Aramus vociferus* ("vociferous"), they are now *A. guarauna,* probably for the Warrau people of South America.

Before they were settled in their own family, limpkins had confused ornithologists, because they resemble diverse other birds. Like storks, ibises, and cranes, limpkins don't have webbed feet, stand more often than they swim, and fly with their necks extended. Their looped intestine is like a rail's, and the arrangement of their feathers is like a crane's. At one time they were called "courlans," from the French curlew. They had puzzled Bartram, who wrote, "I cannot determine what genus of European birds to join it with." Limpkins are threatened by human expansion, but at night they still haunt the Florida swamps with their lonely, tortured cries.

# LOON

When we say someone is "crazy as a loon" we are doing the bird an injustice. Its "demoniac laughter," which Henry David Thoreau described, signals its mate through misty reeds and brush, and its crazy dancing when the young are threatened is meant to divert the attention of intruders. The common name "loon," from the Scandinavian *lom,* meaning "lame," describes its floppy helplessness on land but not its highly specialized aquatic prowess.

The loon's scientific name was heatedly disputed across the Atlantic. Linnaeus had given both loons and grebes the name *Colymbus,* from the Greek *kolymbis,* " a diving bird." But although

British and American ornithologists could agree that the birds were different, the British insisted on calling the loon *Colymbus,* and the Americans used the name for grebes. The dispute was settled only when the International Commission of Zoological Nomenclature abolished the name *Colymbus* and called the loon *Gavia,* from the Latin for "aquatic bird."

The four species of loons are the only members of the Gaviidae family. The "common loon," unfortunately less common these days, is *Gavia immer,* from the Latin for "immersing." In Britain they are called divers, in France, *plongeons.*

♫ **The name "loon," from the Scandinavian *lom,* meaning "lame," describes the bird's floppy helplessness on land.**

Loons are almost completely submerged when they swim. Their nests are connected to the water by a slipway, and the one or two hatchlings slide immediately into the water. Equaled only by penguins as swimmers and divers, loons can also fly. Unlike most birds, their bones are solid, and their specific gravity so close to that of water they can sink for long periods. Underwater they can close a valve on their nostrils. Their legs, so unhelpful on land, are set far back on their bodies, buried within the flesh to the top of the ankle (intertarsal) joint.

Loons get airborne by "running" on the surface of a large stretch of water and cannot take off from land. They migrate long distances to and from their northern nesting sites. Their spring nuptial plumage, variations of striped and spotted black and white, is extraordinarily beautiful, enhanced by their bright red eyes.

The yellow-billed loon, *G. adamsii,* is called after Dr. Edward Adams, a member of the search party for Sir John Franklin, whose ship and crew were lost in 1847 looking for the elusive Northwest Passage. Although Adams saw new birds, Franklin and his men were not found.

On Walden Pond Thoreau chased a loon, which cried strangely "as if calling on the god of the loons to aid him," and immediately misty rain fell. It seemed to Thoreau "his god was angry with me," so, he wrote, "I left him." Loons are shy birds and, gods or no gods, we do best not to disturb them.

# MAGPIE

**W**omen may not like one suggested origin of the magpie's name, since it comes from a perception that females are garrulous: "Mag" is a diminutive of the name Margaret, and from the time of Noah's ark, magpies have had a reputation for chattering. Magpies were said to be the only creatures that would not go into the ark, preferring to perch on the roof chattering while the world around it drowned.

Shakespeare called this bird a "Magot Pie." Magpies often perch on the backs of cattle to eat insects, or maggots, another possible derivation of their name. Other suggestions abound. One is that the "pie" part of the name comes from magpies collecting objects (especially shiny ones) to make a sundry "pie" of them. The common magpie is black and white, or "pied." Origins of names are hard to pin down, but the simplest and most likely origin of "pie" seems to be from *pica*, Latin for "magpie"! The French name for magpie is *pie*.

In the seventeenth century another English name for this bird was piannet, thought by some to come from a combination of "pie," and "Nanny," a diminutive of the woman's name Agnes.

♫ **From the time of Noah's ark, magpies have had a reputation for chattering.**

One wonders sometimes if such etymological unravelings might be a bit of a wild-goose chase (*see* Goose!). The naturalist Thomas Nuttall described the magpies he saw in California, writing in 1836 that "their call was *pait pait*." So it is even possible that the name piannet was simply an imitation of the bird's cry.

The common magpie (*Pica pica*) is the only British magpie, but it (or a very close relative) is also found in North America, where it is called the black-billed magpie, to distinguish it from the yellow-billed magpie, found by Nuttall and called after him, *P. nuttalli*. For nearly thirty years the English Nuttall explored America. His contemporaries said he was "crazy." Richard Henry Dana (who described traveling with Nuttall in *Two Years Before the Mast*) wrote "Why else [should] a rich man . . . leave a Christian country, and come to such a place as California?" Eventually Nuttall (who also has a woodpecker named for him) *had* to return to his "Christian" homeland, because his rich uncle Jonas left him a legacy on the condition that he reside in Britain.

There were no magpies in Ireland until the seventeenth century, when the English introduced them, giving rise to the saying that "Ireland will never be rid of the English while the magpie remains." However, magpies are not easily gotten rid of. In the 1930s they were poisoned in great numbers for damaging crops, but they remain abundant. They must know the secret of survival, if not of the supernatural, and, accordingly, magpies were attributed with magical powers. Meeting them caused good or bad luck, depending on, as the old folk rhyme goes, how many one encountered:

> One for sorrow, two for mirth,
> Three for a wedding, four for a birth.
> Five for silver, six for gold,
> Seven for a secret not to be told.
> Eight for heaven, nine for hell,
> And ten for the devil's own sel'.

Some people still cross their fingers when they see a single magpie——just in case.

# MERLIN

**M**ary, Queen of Scots had a tame merlin. Because of their small size merlins were considered manageable hunting birds for ladies, who hunted as enthusiastically as men did, and sometimes loved their birds too much; medieval nuns were criticized for bringing them into church.

The name "merlin" comes from the French *esmerillon,* the same root as *merle,* "blackbird" (*see* Blackbird). Possibly, merlins were used to hunt blackbirds, or merles (a gourmet food). In medieval falconry a "merlin" was only the female bird. The less popular male was called a "jack." Their scientific name is *Falco columbarius* ("falcon dove"), from the Latin *columba,* "a dove," because they reputedly ate pigeons. In America they are sometimes called pigeon hawks even though they are falcons, not hawks. They eat pigeons as well as other small birds, which they catch on the wing. Chaucer wrote that "the merlioun payneth Hymself ful ofte the larke for to seke." And Thoreau watched while a pigeon hawk "sported with proud reliance in the fields of air," its wings "like the pearly inside of a shell. . . . It was not lonely, but made all the earth lonely beneath it."

Although anything bigger than a pigeon is dangerous for these small birds to handle, they will sometimes rashly tackle much larger prey. Richardson's merlin, *F. columbarius rich-ardsonii,* is named for John Richardson, a Scottish naval surgeon who first identified it in 1827. He was the naturalist on John

**2. Medieval nuns were criticized for bringing merlins into church.**

Franklin's first Arctic expedition to find the Northwest Passage (*see* Loon). The horrors of this trip included murder and cannibalism. Richardson was one of the nine men, out of a party of twenty, who survived, but his tribulations did not prevent him from returning to the Arctic twice more. Some men, like merlins, will pitch themselves against heavy odds.

# MOCKINGBIRD AND CATBIRD

The mockingbird is the state bird of five American states, including Texas. In a 1927 resolution adopting the bird, the Texas legislature chose the (presumably male) mockingbird for being "a fighter for the protection of his home, falling, if need be, in its defense, like any true Texan." Mockingbirds are not intimidated by animals larger than themselves and have been known to attack even eagles and pigs.

Mockingbirds sing with gusto, too. Their song, sung by day and by night, incorporates everything from frog croaks to engine roars and mimicks anything or anyone. About a tenth of their song is mimicry, the rest improvisation, which personalizes each bird's song. Females apparently favor males with extensive repertoires.

The northern mockingbird is *Mimus polyglottos,* from the Latin *mimus,* "a mimic," and the Greek *poluglottos,* many tongued." The English word "mock" comes from the Late Latin *muccare,* meaning to "wipe one's nose," or "mock," a timeless gesture of scorn. American Indian names for the mockingbird included *cencontlatolly,* meaning "four hundred tongues," and *hushi balbaka,* or "bird that speaks a foreign language." The Cherokees once fed mockingbird hearts to their children to help them learn speech.

Early settlers in America called mockingbirds and catbirds "thrushes" and compared them to European nightingales. Nightingales are not related to catbirds and mockingbirds, though they *are* versatile musicians, as are thrashers, the third member of the Mimidae family. Ornithologists once argued seriously over whether the Old World nightingale or the New World mockingbird had the "better" song. The Honorable Daines Barrington (with whom Gilbert White corresponded) made a speech on the subject to the Royal Society in London. Barrington comfortably concluded that "almost all travellers agree, that the concert in the European woods is superior to that of the other parts of the globe." For the American side, John Audubon made it clear that the nightingale would have to

"study under a MOZART [to] in time, become interesting. . . . But to compare her . . . [to] the Mockingbird, is, . . . quite absurd."

The catbird gets its English name by emitting a mewing sound that Alexander Wilson charmingly compared to "some vagrant orphan kitten . . . bewildered among the briars." The gray cat-bird's former name, given by Linnaeus and still found in some bird books, was *Galeoscoptes carolinensis*. The Greek *gale* means "polecat" (*skopto* means "to jeer or scoff"). The Greeks didn't keep cats as pets but did keep pet polecats (a kind of weasel). Linnaeus must have used *gale* as the nearest Greek equivalent to "cat," thus losing the original reason for the catbird's name; polecats could be pets, but they don't mew like cats—or cat-birds. Although *carolinensis* means "from Carolina," the catbird ranges widely through north American states. The mockingbird lives farther south.

> The word "mock" comes from the Late Latin *muccare,* meaning to "wipe one's nose," a timeless gesture of scorn.

The expression to "sit in the catbird seat" means to be in a high, commanding seat. The radio announcer Red Barber popu-larized the southern expression when commentating on baseball games. However, it would be more accurate to say the "mock-ingbird seat," because catbirds shyly hide in shrubs, whereas mockingbirds often sing from on high. The catbird's present name is *Dumetella carolinensis,* from the Latin *dumentum,* "bush," because catbirds inhabit low bushes.

In Harper Lee's 1960 southern novel, *To Kill a Mockingbird,* two young children (the little girl still in second grade!) are given air rifles. They are warned not to shoot mockingbirds, which "don't do one thing but sing their hearts out for us. That's why it's a sin to kill a mockingbird."

# NIGHTINGALE

Izaak Walton wrote in *The Compleat Angler* that the nightingale's song "might make mankind to think miracles are not ceased." Although there are no nightingales in the New World, most Americans are familiar with the idea of the nightingale's beautiful song. Settlers in America first nostalgically called mockingbirds "nightingales," later arguing over which bird had the more beautiful song (*see* Mockingbird).

Nightingales sing magically in the darkness of night. Their English name comes from the Anglo-Saxon *niht,* "night," and *galen,* "a singer." Portia, in *The Merchant of Venice,* says "The nightingale, if she should sing by day / . . . would be thought / No better musician than the wren." Actually nightingales can sing all night *and* through the next day too, and although Shakespeare wrote "she," it is the males, not the females, who sing. Females arrive after the males at their European breeding sites, and this can be any time during the day or night. So the males sing constantly to attract them to their established territory. As soon as nesting begins, they stop singing.

In old literature the nightingale was often called Philomel, after the daughter of Pandion (*see* Osprey). Philomela's brother-in-law Tereus raped her, then cut out her tongue so she couldn't tell what he had done. However, she wove her story into a tapestry for her sister Procne to see, and the two of them took revenge on Tereus by killing and cooking his son Itys, whom he unwittingly ate. These charmless characters were all turned into birds by the Greek gods. Procne became a nightingale and Philomela a sparrow, but they were somehow reversed in the Roman version of the story, in which the tongueless Philomela became a nightin-

**♫ In a Roman version of a Greek myth, the tongueless Philomela, the daughter of Pandion, became a nightingale and could then sing.**

gale. Perhaps that was considered the only way she could hope to tell her story (although she would also have had to change her sex).

Imposed onto this tale was an Eastern legend in which the nightingale could only sing by pressing her breast against a thorn, often coloring a rose with her blood. This was usually for the sake of unrequited love, and the bleeding nightingale subsequently expired, explaining very adequately why the song was not always considered cheery. Many poets have written about the nightingale's song, sometimes calling it a source of joy, sometimes one of sadness. Samuel Taylor Coleridge got the bird's sex right, writing that the nightingale sings as if "fearful that an April night / Would be too short for him to utter forth / His love-chart."

The Eurasian nightingale's name is *Luscinia megarhynchos. Lucus* is Latin for a "woody grove," often sacred. *Megas* means "big" and *rhynchos* "bill," more probably describing the volume of sound that pours out of it, rather than the bill itself, which isn't particularly large.

It is said that in Havering-at-Bower, in Essex, there were no nightingales after the eleventh century. King Edward the Confessor did not appreciate the nightingales' songs, which interrupted his meditations. He prayed that these songs might never be heard there again, and his prayer was answered.

# NUTHATCH

T

he nuthatch," wrote Christian Ludwig Brehm in 1822, "not only climbs up trees quite as nimbly as the woodpeckers, but also . . . climbs down, often hanging head downward. . . . How did the Creator manage this?"

Brehm was much respected in his time and published the first ornithological journal, which came out several times a year and consisted of six to twelve pages on "the newest and most important in bird lore." He was notable for not merely observing birds but carefully examining them. Answering his rhetorical question about the Creator's capabilities, he wrote, "since the arrangement of climbing equipment in the nuthatch is so different from that of the woodpeckers, its way of climbing is also very different." The nuthatch's toes spread out, observed Brehm "almost as far apart as the body is long," with "needle-pronged claws," and "a number of pads below." Another difference is the soft tail feathers, which can't be used as a brace, as in woodpeckers, but don't therefore limit the nuthatches to vertical climbing.

The nuthatch's family name, Sittidae, comes from the Greek for "a climbing bird" and was used by Aristotle. The common name, nuthatch, has nothing to do with hatching nuts (or eggs) but comes from the Anglo-Saxon *hnuta,* "a nut," and the Old English *hakken* or *hacken,* meaning "to break" or "cleave." These little birds will wedge a nut into a crevice to hold it while they pound it open. In 1871, Gilbert White wrote that he "often placed nuts in the chink of a gate-post" and watched nuthatches open them "with a rapping noise that may be heard at a considerable distance." He also called them "jar birds."

> **The nuthatch's family name, Sittidae, comes from the Greek for "a climbing bird."**

Their French name is *torchepot,* which is the same as "mud dauber," a name used in southern England. Nuthatches prefer taking over nest holes made by woodpeckers—which are better equipped to excavate them—but they often make the entrance hole smaller by building a mud rim around it. White-breasted nuthatches have been seen "bill-sweeping," or holding crushed blister beetles in their beak and scouring the entrance to the nest hole, presumably to deter rodents.

Nuthatches have the vocal equipment to sing well but don't really use it. They spend most of their lives scurrying up and down trees for insects or wedging nuts into crevices, often for future use, and don't seem to have time to perch and sing. It seems somehow appropriate that when they do finally stop to sleep they roost head downward, as if too exhausted to perch right side up.

# ORIOLE

It was not unusual for ancient medical cures to be associated with color absorption, such as wrapping a patient in a red blanket to take away a fever's fiery heat. The Old World oriole's Greek name was *ikteros,* meaning "jaundice." Pliny the Elder told of a jaundiced man seeing an oriole that was the color of his ailment. Immediately the man was cured and the bird died.

Early American naturalists, both for nostalgia and because birds were as yet unnamed, were apt to call birds that looked familiar after the ones back home, especially if their habits seemed similar. This is why the bird's common name, oriole, on both sides of the Atlantic, is from *aureolus,* Latin for "golden," even though the birds aren't related. The Greek name *ikteros* (or Icterus) also crossed the Atlantic and was applied to the American oriole's family, formerly the Icteridae (*see* Blackbird). But the Old World orioles are in the Oriolidae family.

All orioles build beautiful hanging nests, using their feet as well as their bills to construct them. They eat fruit and seeds as well as insects, and some were considered a pest in the Mediterranean because they ate figs.

In spring Baltimore orioles come to the United States from the tropics to breed. They often use man-made materials for their nests, so the ornithologist Alexander Wilson warned women to keep "narrowly watching their thread that may chance to be out bleaching." The Baltimore oriole's name, wrote Mark Catesby in his eighteenth-century book *Natural History of the Carolinas* "comes from the Lord Baltimore's coat of arms." The lord was governor of Maryland, and the coat of arms was described as "Paly of six, Topaz and Diamond, a Bend, counterchang'd," in the same colors as the bird's plumage.

**Orioles were once thought to cure jaundice.**

Scott's oriole, *Icterus parisorum,* was given its scientific name by Napoleon's nephew Charles Bonaparte. *Parisorum* was to honor the Paris brothers, French businessmen who sent natural history specimens from Mexico. General Darius Couch (*see* Kingbird) gave this oriole its common name for General Winfield Scott, with whom he had campaigned in Mexico. Scott was general in chief of the army until 1861, when he retired. He was nicknamed "Old Fuss and Feathers" (because he was so punctilious) and orioles do migrate to Mexico, but other than these incidentals the man seems to have had no avian connections at all. He doesn't mention birds in his two-volume autobiography, and unlike his contemporary Emily Dickinson, it appears he really didn't care if

> To hear an Oriole sing
> May be a common thing
> Or only a divine.

# OSPREY

Ospreys are the only raptors that dive into water. They hover high until they spot a fish, then suddenly plummet into the water to catch it. The common name "osprey" comes from the Latin *ossifragus,* "bone breaker," which isn't really apt, because these birds swallow fish whole or tear off chunks of the flesh. Ospreys were probably once confused with lammergeier vultures, which do break bones (*see* Vulture).

The osprey's scientific name is *Pandion haliaetus,* given by Linnaeus, who thought they were a kind of eagle. *Haliaetus* means "sea hawk." Pandion was a legendary king of Attica. His family life was not ideal: two of his three tragic daughters were changed into birds (*see* Nightingale), and his nasty son-in-law Tereus became a hawk. If Pandion was almost the only member of this unhappy family who *wasn't* turned into a bird, perhaps he was also the only one whose character was worthy of his status.

**Some thought ospreys cast a spell on fish.** Maybe Linnaeus named the kingly osprey as a tribute to Pandion's majesty, rather than to commemorate his sad story. Ospreys were moved from the falcon family to one of their own, the Pandionidae, by the French naturalist Marie-Jules-César LeLorgne de Savigny, who accompanied Napoleon to Egypt. He was distinguished for meticulously naming numerous insect mouthparts!

The osprey's feet have spiky pads, called spicules, which enable the bird to keep a firm grasp on fish. When airborne, the osprey turns the fish to carry it headfirst. This reduces air friction as the osprey flies. In the days when birds of prey were trained to hunt, ospreys were sometimes tamed, but no one could stop them from carrying their catch out of reach to a nearby tree, where they swallowed the fish headfirst, so that fins and tail slid down more easily.

Ospreys are such good fishers that some thought they cast a spell on fish. In George Peele's sixteenth-century play *The Battle of Alcazar,* fish shall "turn their glistering bellies up," for the "princely ospraie" to catch and give to "the Moore's" wife. A Baptist missionary explorer, George Henry Loskiel, still believed in 1794 that the osprey "possesses a power of alluring the fish toward the surface, by means of an oily substance contained in its body" and that if this oil is smeared on bait, fish will find it "impossible" to resist.

Simon Pokagon, chief of the Pottawattume tribe of Michigan, wrote about the osprey. This respected nineteenth-century ornithologist camouflaged his clothes with sprays of flowers to watch one from beside a lake. He was also interested in names, and once said that Indian names "should never be translated in English," giving as an example the name of the city of Chicago, which came from the Indian word for skunk! However, he spent much of his energy trying to get the American government to pay his tribe for land bought and developed into that city. He called the "Kegon Penay-segant Win-ge-see," or osprey, a "clean industrious bird . . . living . . . through its own skill and labors," and contrasted it with the eagle, the national bird of America (*see* Eagle), which, he pointed out, often steals the osprey's catch. The American government took so long to make good on its contract with the Pottawattumes that one wonders if, when Simon Pokagon wrote about the osprey and the eagle, he was thinking only about birds.

# OSTRICH

Politicians, wishing to criticize eruditely (a political talent not much in demand these days), could safely call rivals *struthonian,* meaning that, like foolish ostriches, they refuse to acknowledge reality. Ostriches were once believed to hide from the dangers of reality by burying their heads in the sand, thus leaving their bodies exposed. *Struthio* is the Greek for ostrich. The Romans called the ostrich *avis struthio* ("ostrich bird"), which became *avestruz* in Spanish and "ostrich" in English. Actually ostriches *don't* bury their heads in sand, although they sometimes stretch them forward and rest them on the ground. They do have a reputation for stupidity, and they have very small brains: It took six hundred ostrich brains (on the half shell?) to satisfy the culinary demands of the Roman emperor, Elagabalus!

The scientific name for ostrich is *Struthio camelus.* Like camels, ostriches are adapted to the desert. They hardly ever need to drink, and their nasal glands eliminate salt from brackish water. Luscious black lashes shade their eyes from the sun. Native to Africa, ostriches could also be found in Arabia until the twentieth century.

The prophet Job said the ostrich "leaveth her eggs on the earth . . . where the foot may crush them," and in the book of Lamentations the daughters of Zion are called "cruel like the ostriches in the wilderness," because ostriches were thought to be bad parents. Actually, these biblical perceptions were wrong. Ostrich eggs are hard to break from the outside and can withstand the weight of a three-hundred-pound brooding parent. But they are fragile against impact from *inside,* and the nascent ostrich shatters the shell apart, rather than neatly pecking it open, like most hatching chicks. Although ostriches are the largest living birds, their huge eggs, the biggest on earth, are the smallest in proportion to the adult's size. Most females lay one egg in a communal nest in the sand and then go on their way. One dominant female,

> In the book of Lamentations the daughters of Zion are called "cruel like the ostriches in the wilderness," because ostriches were thought to be bad parents.

however, takes the day shift for incubation, camouflaged by her sandy-colored feathers. The male incubates at night, protected by his black feathers. After the eggs hatch, the male looks after the young by himself, for up to six months.

Ostrich plumes (the primary feathers from the male's tail and wings) were an ancient symbol of justice, because they are symmetrically divided on each side of a central shaft. They have no stiff edge, and because they are unbarbed and fluffy, the plumes were used decoratively. By the nineteenth century ostrich farmers, called "feather barons," harvested tons of ostrich plumes for fashionable hats. After World War I, even though the plumes were farmed without killing the birds, large feathered hats went out of style, and the market collapsed.

Ostriches lack a "keeled" (or V-shaped) breastbone, needed to support the flying muscles, and so they and their kind are called *ratites,* from the Latin "raft," or "flat-bottomed boat." They use their wings like sails to gain speeds of about fifty miles per hour. Their distinctive foot, with all but two toes fused together, is adapted to running over sand. It is also used as a powerful weapon.

Ostriches will eat anything, from the stones they need to aid their digestion to watches or strands of wire. Once they were thought to eat only iron, and in heraldry they were depicted holding a nail. Curious birds indeed, but their oddities suit their unique way of life.

# Owl

An owl's cry, wrote John Ruskin, "whatever wise people may say," is "always prophetic of mischief." Owls were often associated with evil, and their diet of snakes, frogs, and rodents frequently formed the ingredients of ancient recipes with unpleasing purposes—as in *Macbeth*. Adam's first wife, Lilith, the "daughter of howling," who gave birth to demons, was an owl—*yanshoof* in Hebrew.

In ancient Greece the owl was Athena's bird, considered lucky rather than ill-omened. Diodorus Siculus described how the Greek commander Agathocles "let loose into the army in many places owls, [which] . . . settling on the shields and helmets encouraged the soldiers." Large bubo owls sometimes seem as if they are leading troops of birds, and one old name for them was "grand duke." They are really trying to escape the attentions of small birds who, recognizing an enemy, gang up on a sleepily digesting owl and mob it.

The common name "owl" comes from the Old English *ule,*

describing their howl, or from *ulula* in Latin. Sometimes what seems to be one cry are two cries, from owls answering each other. Gilbert White wrote that the owls of Selbourne "hoot in three different keys." Many of their names (like *Otus, Asio,* and *Bubo*), mean "owl" in Latin or Greek. A few are called after people, like the tiny elf owl, *Micrathene whitneyi,* named for Josiah Dwight Whitney, who led a geological survey in California (where the famous mountain also bears his name). *Micrathene* means "Athena's small bird," and *Athene* owls are all small.

**♀ Owls fly soundlessly because the edges of their wings are fluffy.**

All owls except barn and bay owls are in the Strigidae family, from the Latin, *strix,* "screech." Members of the Tytonidae, or barn owl family (from *tuto,* Latin for "owl") generally have flat, heart-shaped faces, forming a receptor that bounces sound to the two ears, which are of different heights. This helps them pinpoint the origin of the faintest rustle, so they can then pounce through leaves or snow to extricate quivering rodents. Owls fly soundlessly because the edges of their wings are fluffy rather than stiff. They swallow their prey whole, ejecting the undigestible portions in pellets.

Bay owls, also in the Tytonidae family, are named *Phodilus,* meaning in Greek, "afraid of light," reflecting a traditional belief that owls cannot see in daylight. In fact they can, although they see particularly well in the dark. Their night vision comes from extra-long light-gathering rods in their eyes, making their eye-balls tubular rather than round. They can't roll their eyes, so they have to eerily turn their whole heads to look around. They generally hunt in the crepuscular hours of dawn and dusk.

Owls often coexist with humans, eating rodents, which thrive around people too. The Bible predicted that human civilization would fall, leaving "wasted land," with ruined palaces, overrun with nettles and brambles. It is comforting (at least for bird lovers), that this prophesy describes "a court for owls" remaining in the midst of the desolation.

# PARROT

Prostitutes in India reputedly carried parrots, and one of the sixty-four practices required in the *Kama Sutra* was teaching a parrot to talk. A sailor traveling with Alexander the Great brought home a parrot, and Aristotle described a bird "from India" that had a tongue like a man and "became more loquacious when it drank wine." A parrot charmed Julius Caesar by saying "Hail, Caesar," and Ovid wrote a dirge for a pet parrot destined for avian paradise.

Parrots are Psittacidae, derived from *bittakos,* which was the Greek rendition of the bird's Indian name. The common name "parrot" is from *Perroquet,* a diminutive of the French name Pierre, often used for a priest. According to the sixteenth-century naturalist Pierre Belon, large parrots were *papegaux.* The birds were popular props of clowns, and no doubt were used to make fun of the church. A popinjay, which means someone of gaudy dress and empty phrases, comes from *babbaga,* Arabic for "parrot," now "pappagallo" in Italian.

Many new kinds of parrots were brought back to Europe from the Americas and Australia. The macaw's common name comes from the Portuguese *macao,* a West Indian palm tree whose fruit parrots there eat. *Anodorhynchus,* the first part of the hyacinth macaw's scientific name, *Anodorhynchus hyacinthus,* means "without teeth." No birds have teeth, but some have notched bills; this macaw does not. Its bill, the upper part of which is not attached to its skull and hinges upward, is immensely strong. Macaws feed on otherwise toxic seeds, which they can digest by eating clay. *Hyacinthus* refers to the bird's brilliant blue plumage. This parrot comes from Brazil, where Alfred Russel Wallace, in the mid-nineteenth century, explained a technique to change the color of a macaw's feathers by plucking a patch of skin bare and rubbing poison into it. If the bird survived, the new feathers would not be blue but bright red or orange, more valued for adornment.

In 1606 Spanish explorers in Australia described white parrots with yellow crests and black feet and bills. These were sulfur-crested cockatoos, now popular pets. Their name, *Cacatua galerita,* is from the Malayan *kakatoe* and *galeritus,* the Latin for "wearing a hood."

Most parrots come from South America, and Brazil was once called Terra Papagalli (Land of the Parrots). North American settlers found only small parrots, Carolina parakeets, which the explorer Antoine Du Pratz called *Papagai à tête aurore,* "parrots with dawn-tinted heads." They "speak little," he wrote in 1774, and "a silent parrot would never make its fortune among our French ladies." Not only did the Carolina

**Ovid wrote a dirge for a pet parrot.**

parakeet fail to makes its fortune, it became extinct. Audubon wrote that it "destroys every kind of fruit indiscriminately," and the farmer "commits great slaughter among them." The remaining parakeets, "as if conscious of the death of their companions, sweep over their bodies," where they continued to be shot down.

Parrots can live nearly a century, and Alexander von Humboldt, visiting the tombs of a lost South American tribe in 1818, wrote that "an old parrot was shown at Maypures, of which the inhabitants related they did not understand what it said, because it spoke the language of the [extinct] Atures." But more often we outlive parrots rather than they us, and too many wild parrots are still captured for the lucrative talking-pet market. Tame parrots learn to speak with uncanny accuracy, and can even be taught to count. No wonder they were thought to be the original companions of Adam. Columbus, when he first found them, believed he had discovered Paradise.

# PARTRIDGE

Real partridges are not native to America. The first known attempt to import them was by Richard Bache, Benjamin Franklin's son-in-law, who brought them to his plantation on the Delaware River, but it was not until the early 1900s, when they were taken west, that they really flourished.

They were game birds in ancient Asia and Greece, and the Romans called them *perdix,* which meant "partridge." In Old French it was *pertriz,* and in Old English, *pertriche.* Because the Greek *perdesthein* means "to fart," one etymologist has suggested that "partridge" is "echoic of the noise [these birds] made on taking flight when startled." In military terms a "partridge" is a charge of cannons fired together—which does not necessarily negate the same postulated root.

When miles of hedges were planted to enclose British fields during the eighteenth century, partridges, which hide in underbrush, flourished. They became favorite gun birds and were mostly shot on the ground, but by the nineteenth century the French sport of shooting birds on the wing became customary.

Guns and ammunition had improved, and partridges could easily be flushed out of their hiding places and shot as they flew into the air. One English aristocrat recorded the deaths of 10,744 partridges in his personal shooting journal. A "brace" of partridge, or a pair of birds, comes from the Latin *bracchia,* "arms," as does "embrace," usually done with two arms.

**It is unlikely that the partridge sent to "my true love" was for a dining treat.**

The "partridge in a pear tree" in the Christmas song, *must* have been a red-legged partridge, *Alectoris rufa* (from *alektor,* "cock," and *rufa,* "red"), first introduced to Britain in the reign of Charles II. The common, or gray partridge (*Perdix perdix*), native to Britain, never perches in trees (even in pear trees).

The partridge-shooting season began in August and ended in the autumn. Even before the era of legal shooting seasons, it seems unlikely that the partridge sent to "my true love" on the "first day of Christmas" was for a dining treat. By Christmastime, partridges are generally considered to be inedibly tough. However, according to Bartolemeo Sacchi, known as Platina, who wrote on the topic in 1468, eating partridge "arouses the half-extinct desire for venereal pleasures." Pear trees, according to the seventeenth-century *Herbal* of Nicolas Culpeper, "belong to Venus." So even if the traditional present might be gastronomically out of season, it clearly could send another message.

# PEACOCK

"Happening to make a visit to my neighbour's peacocks," wrote Gilbert White in one of his famous eighteenth-century letters from Selborne, "I could not help observing that the trains of these magnificent birds appear by no means to be their tails." He explained that the real tail is a "range of short brown stiff feathers" that supports the male's showy fan feathers. This fan is set so far forward that only the bird's head and neck are visible in front of it, and when peacocks mate these huge colored feathers "clatter like the swords of a sword-dancer."

Peacocks are lekking birds. "Lek" comes from the Swedish *leka*, "to play" (in all senses). When lekking, the males parade on a cleared "court," and the females cluster around those that make the best show. Some males in the lek don't mate, but they have a better chance of doing so if they hang around, much as aspiring humans might frequent a bar hoping for a stray date.

♪ **The male's bloodcurdling scream, believed once to be despair at the ugliness of his feet, is really a warning cry.**

King Solomon may have received peacocks along with "gold, silver, ivory and apes" (although the translation of "peacock" is sometimes questioned by scholars). We do know the Phoenicians kept them. The peacock was also the goddess Juno's favorite bird, used for watching out (with its many feathery eyes) for her husband's infidelities.

The Christian church adopted the peacock as a symbol of vigilance and expanded the range of sins to watch out for. Peacocks are depicted in many religious paintings. The birds were sacred to the Hindus too, perhaps because the peacock's courting season corresponded with the longed-for rainy season. Peacocks continued to be associated with rain, as in the English proverb:

When the peacock loudly bawls
Soon we'll have both rain and squalls.

The peacock's flesh, according to a twelfth-century bestiary, "is so hard that it is scarcely subject to putrefaction." This belief gave peacocks a reputation for immortality, but they were eaten anyway. After a banquet of peacocks, medieval knights took an oath of allegiance invoking "God, the Virgin, the Ladies and the Peacock." The Romans ate them with less reverence: peacocks' tongues and peas with gold shavings were included in the tasty banquets of the emperor Elagabalus.

The name "peacock" has nothing to do with peas. The domesticated peacock, *Pavo cristatus,* originated in southern India and Sri Lanka, where the Dravidian language, Tamil, was spoken. In Tamil the peacock was *tokei,* which Arab traders corrupted to *tawus.* This in Greek became *pfau,* and in Latin *pavo.* The Old English was *pawe,* which became *pocock,* and then "peacock."

We accuse the peacock of vanity, but the male's clumsy tail is really a heavy burden he bears in the cause of reproduction. His bloodcurdling scream, believed once to be despair at the ugliness of his feet, is really a warning cry. But it has not always saved him from predators, or from people.

# PELICAN

A wonderful bird is the pelican,
His bill will hold more than his belican.
He can take in his beak
Food enough for a week,
But I'm damned if I see how the helican.

Dixon Lanier Merritt, the twentieth-century southern journalist, rightly marveled at the wondrousness of the pelican but gave a false impression of its bill. It *does* hold a lot, over three gallons, but of water, not fish. The bird scoops up water and fish together into the gular pouch attached to the rim of the lower mandible, then ejects the water and swallows the fish. The pouch is never filled for any length of time with food.

Pelicans also use their pouches to hold regurgitated fishy soup to feed their chicks. To get at this, the chicks dive deep inside the pouch, which rests against the parent's breast. This behavior probably accounts for the legend that young pelicans drank blood from a self-inflicted wound in their mother's breast. In the legend, the chicks die but are revived three days later with this blood. And the pelican was a symbol of Christ's resurrection, often depicted in religious paintings or ecclesiastical coats of arms; Dante refers to "Christ, our Pelican." It is possible that pelicans were confused with flamingos, which do feed their young regurgitated "milk," bloody red from carotenoids in their diet (*see* Flamingo). The name "pelican," which comes from the Greek *pelekus*, "axe," once described any bird with a large bill, including woodpeckers and flamingos. Another early name was *alcatraz* (*see* Albatross).

Two members of the Pelecanidae family breed in North America. The brown pelican, *Pelecanus occidentalis*, "from the western hemisphere," dives into the sea for fish. White pelicans feed in shallow water, sometimes cooperatively walking in U formation to trap fish. Their name, *P. erythrorhynchos*, means "red-billed." During breeding season the orange bill develops a bony crest, which later falls off.

In 1662 the Russian ambassador presented a pair of Dalmation pelicans to Charles II for his exotic bird collection in St. James's Park. *Dalmacija* was a Croatian region along the Adriatic coast. The Dalmation pelican, *P. crispus* (meaning "curly"), has a wavy crest on its head and is darker gray than the pelican known to the ancients, *P. onocrotalus,* whose name comes from the Greek *onos,* "donkey," referring to the braying sound of young pelicans. The adults are usually silent.

Although pelicans are a symbol of sorrowful solitude in the Bible ("I am like a pelican of the wilderness"), they often nest in tight groups. Usually only one of the chicks in each nest is reared; the other is neglected by the parents or killed by its sibling.

♪ The pelican was a symbol of Christ's resurrection; Dante refers to "Christ, our Pelican."

During World War I, Florida fishermen suspected pelicans of depleting their fishing grounds. There was a war effort to eat more fish, and federal protection of pelicans was almost withdrawn. A party of ornithologists led by Gilbert Pearson made 3,428 pelicans regurgitate their food, and found that only twenty-seven of the fish they had eaten were the kind humans eat. So the pelicans were saved!

# PENGUIN

Penguins get their common name from the now extinct great auks, seabirds that weren't related to them but had white bellies and black backs and walked upright on land. Sailors called the auks "penguins." The sixteenth-century historian Richard Hakluyt told of a Welsh lord, Madoc Gwineth, who stopped at Penguin Island off Newfoundland, named the birds from the Welsh *pen,* "head," and *gwyn,* "white," and continued his journey to "discover" America. A more probable origin of the name (obviously preferred by later English historians) is the Latin *pinguis,* or "fat." In cold areas, up to a third of a penguin's weight is blubber, although penguins inhabiting the southern coasts of Africa, Australia, and the Galápagos have mechanisms for *losing* heat.

At the end of the sixteenth century sailors off Patagonia saw birds similar to northern auks, which they called "pengwins." Southern pengwins and northern auks shared the name "penguin" until the last two great auks were shot, on June 4, 1844, and the only "penguins" left were in the Southern Hemisphere.

Adélie penguins were named by nineteenth-century explorer Jules Dumont d'Urville in honor of his wife. This "obscure ensign" (as he called himself) was credited with the discovery of the *Venus de Milo*. His navy career advanced rapidly, and soon he commanded his own ship, the *Astrolabe,* which sailed to "a silent world in which everything threatens the destruction of one's faculties," wrote Dumont. The *Pygoscelis adeliae* derived the first part of its name from Greek *puge skelos,* "rump-legged," referring to the legs set far back on the body, which steer penguins in the water but cause their ungainly walk on land. They use their strong, short wings to "fly" underwater.

**In cold areas, up to a third of a penguin's weight is blubber, and a probable origin of the name is the Latin *pinguis,* or "fat."**

The two biggest penguins, the emperor and the king, were found by Johann Reinhold Forster, the naturalist on Captain Cook's expedition to the Antarctic on the *Endeavour* in the 1770s. Forster worked so hard that he sometimes had to rinse his "whole body in a cask of sea water" to wake himself up and write his notes. He named the king penguin after King George III. Apparently the gesture did not make much of an impression, because the Admiralty did not pay him, and he ended up in debtor's prison until rescued by his son. Both emperor and king penguins were *Aptenodytes patagonica,* but later the emperor penguin was renamed *A. forsteri* in Foster's honor.

The prefix is from the Greek *a ptenos,* "without wings," and *dutes,* "a diver."

The male emperor penguin incubates the single egg on its feet, holding it against a bare brood patch on its abdomen and eating nothing for months, huddling with the other devoted fathers throughout a winter of perpetual frozen nights and swirling blizzards. If, after months away, the female's return with food is delayed, the male feeds the chick "milk" from his crop while they both wait.

Even sailors, who once heartlessly slaughtered penguins, cramming them into ship's holds by the thousands, must have been touched by the birds. John Winter, who sailed with Francis Drake to Patagonia in 1578, described penguins walking "so upright, that a farre off man would take them to be little children."

# PETREL

Petrels don't walk on water, although their name probably comes from the account of Saint Peter walking on the stormy waters of Lake Gennesaret. When petrels, especially storm petrels, fly close to the surface of the sea, they push themselves along with their feet, looking as if they are walking on the waves. An old name for petrel was "pitterel," and their common name could come from this "pattering," or "pittering," on the sea.

Storm petrels are in their own family, Hydrobatidae (from *hydros,* "water," and *batein,* "tread over"). These small, dark birds often seek shelter in the lee or wake of ships during storms. Sailors called them Mother Carey's chickens and feared that their appearance was indicative of bad weather. "Mother Carey" could be a sailor's prayer to *Madre cara,* or "dear Mother." As far as we know, this name was first used by the crew of the *Swallow,* commanded by Philip Carteret in the 1760s, during a grueling thirty-one-month voyage on which over half the crew died.

The Procellariidae family includes petrels, as well as shearwaters, prions, and fulmars, all pelagic birds that spend most of their lives at sea. *Procella* is Latin for "storm." They swim and fly well, and some have wing spans several feet wide. Birds in this family are called tubenoses, because of two nostrils along the top of their bills. These nostrils, sometimes quite prominent, like double-barreled rifles, are connected to glands that excrete salt from the seawater they drink.

Shearwaters, as the name suggests, cut along the tops of waves. Some shearwaters are called *Puffinus* (*see* Puffin). The name "prion" comes from the Greek word for "serrated," describing this bird's bill. Prions have soft, dense feathers and are sometimes called Antarctic doves. Humans have always been eager to bestow their own names on anything, from libraries to worm species, and ornithologists, being no exception, have about fifteen species of Procellariidae named after them. Some of these species are very alike, in varying colors of gray, white, black, and brown, and only experts can distinguish between them.

Petrels have webbed feet, and the legs of some are so weak they can't stand but must push themselves along on their breasts when they go ashore to nest. Many nest in burrows, and most

**Fulmar petrels, which eject fishy vomit, got their name from the Old Norse *ful,* "foul," and *mar,* "gull," because of their pervasive smell.**

leave their chick before it is fully fledged. The chick is fat enough to exist alone before growing feathers and leaving the nest. When caught and eaten, these fat chicks were once called "mutton-birds." Both chicks and parents defend themselves by ejecting fishy vomit. The fulmar petrels got their name from the Old Norse *ful,* "foul," and *mar,* "gull," because of this habit and the pervasive smell of the birds and their nests.

Some petrels can smell dimethyl sulfide, which is given off by krill, from long distances away. Petrels eat not only krill but any rotting fish or carcass they find. Sometimes whalers could barely get them off the decks after a kill. They ate until they were too heavy to fly, then vomited to get airborne. After these bulimic orgies, they might soar for days, gracefully dipping and dancing through crested waves. No wonder horrifed sailors called petrels "devil-birds," then later prayed to the gracious beauty of the same birds, for comfort in a storm.

# PHALAROPE

Phalaropes are small aquatic birds that have mixed characteristics of ducks, sandpipers, and coots but differ from them in their mating behavior. They breed in northern latitudes, migrating long distances south in winter. Unlike many birds, the female arrives at the breeding grounds first and stakes out the nesting territory. When the male arrives it is the female, resplendent in nuptial plumage, who aggressively courts and chases the drabber male, fighting with other females to get him. The hen-pecked male phalarope is more than passably domesticated: He builds the nest, incubates the eggs, and raises the young, while the female leaves him to it, often pursuing another male. Ornithologists explain this behavior by suggesting that where food is scarce and predators common, females, in effect, "free" themselves to ensure that the species has a better chance of survival.

Phalaropes, like ducks, have downy breasts, and they are very buoyant. They can't dive, but they sometimes upend to feed, like dabbling ducks. Their bills are long and thin, like those of sandpipers. In still water they "pirouette" in counterclockwise circles, paddling with their feet to stir up mosquito larvae. The first part of the phalarope's scientific name, *Phalaropus,* comes from the Greek *phalaris,* "coot," and *pous,* "foot," because of their partially webbed, lobed feet (*see* Coot).

**♀ Female Wilson's phalaropes sometimes keep company with male ducks—while the male phalaropes and female ducks raise their respective young.**

Wilson's phalarope is *P. tricolor,* and the female has a beautiful nuptial plumage of three colors—white, black, and reddish brown. Alexander Wilson did not live long enough to complete his *American Ornithology,* and the ninth volume was finished by George Ord. In it Ord calls a phalarope *wilsonii,* explaining that Wilson's description was "so scrawled and obscured that parts of the writing were not legible." However, the bird had already been given its scientific name earlier, and tricolor could not be changed to *wilsonii.* But it is still commonly called "Wilson's phalarope."

Female Wilson's phalaropes are sometimes seen during the breeding season keeping company with male ducks—while the male phalaropes and female ducks are occupied raising their respective young. How all this contributes to "species survival" is still an interesting field of study. But in contemporary human terms at least, it appears to be a pleasantly carefree arrangement.

# PHEASANT

"The slim little chick was greyish-brown with dark markings, and it was the most alive little spark of a creature. . . . So tiny and so utterly without fear!" D. H. Lawrence's description is of a pheasant chick, hatched by a domestic hen. The bird would serve to spark a new life and love for Lady Chatterley but was itself being raised to be shot "ultimately by fat men after breakfast."

The first pheasants were probably brought from Asia for their beauty, but they soon became a principal game bird in Europe. The pheasant was too heavy to be taken by birds of prey, which were commonly used for hunting in the Middle Ages, so when guns replaced hawks and falcons, pheasants became common meals. By 1532 Henry VIII had begun the practice of raising pheasants to be let loose and hunted. His accounts include a mention of eleven shillings paid to "the french Preste [priest] the fesaunt breder for to bye him a gowne."

Although Jefferson included pheasants in his plans for a projected "asylum" for wild creatures, they were not permanently introduced to America until the 1880s, when Judge Owen Denny, the United States consul general of Shanghai, shipped several Chinese ring-necked pheasants to be let loose in the Willamette Valley in Oregon. By 1892 these had increased so abundantly that a seventy-five-day hunting season was instigated, and fifty thousand pheasants were killed on its opening day.

The name "pheasant" comes from the classical Phasis Valley in Colchis, now the River Rioni in Georgia. The ring-necked pheasant is *Phasianus colchicus.* Jason returning from his quest for the Golden Fleece was said to have brought pheasants, also golden, back too.

**The name "pheasant" comes from the classical Phasis Valley in Colchis, now the River Rioni in Georgia.**

The exquisite beauty of the male pheasant is, of course, intended to attract females. Males attack each other, and they used to be trapped easily with mirrors, not due to their vanity but because they will run belligerently at the image of a male bird. The male's main job *is* his beauty, for the females generally look after the chicks while the males go off to molt and wait until the next breeding season. They will not all make it back after our hunting season. If the pheasant is only to be shot, then as Alexander Pope put it:

Ah! what avail his glossie, varying Dyes,
His Purple Crest, and Scarlet-circled Eyes,
The vivid Green his shining Plumes unfold;
His painted Wings, and Breast that flames with Gold?

Those who breed pheasants for hunting say that sportsmen are the best conservationists because they keep up the numbers of birds. Even so, Lady Chatterley's chicks are perhaps more affecting still, in their innocent zest for life.

# PHOEBE

I n what John Audubon described as his "youthful days of an American woodsman," he lived at his French father's plantation near Valley Forge, Pennsylvania. In 1806, in a cave where he often sat reading, he noticed a pair of phoebes return-ing to nest, and "in that place, kind reader, . . . I first saw . . . the force of parental affection in birds." More importantly, he then made ornithological history when he "fixed a light silver thread" around the legs of the young birds just before they left the nest. The next year, when phoebes nested not far from the cave, "I had the pleasure of finding that two of them had the little ring on the leg." Banding birds was to become, and still is, perhaps the most important way we have of studying them.

Phoebes are New World "tyrant flycatchers," not related to Old World flycatchers, or Muscicapidae (*see* Flycatcher). But Audubon did not distinguish them and gave his eastern phoebe the scientific name *Muscicapa fusca* ("dark flycatcher"). When Thomas Say discovered another new phoebe in Colorado,

Charles Bonaparte named it *Muscicapa saya,* in honor of Say, "a naturalist of whom America may justly be proud, and whose talents and knowledge are only equalled by his modesty." Thomas Say was interested in more than birds; in 1828 he completed a three-volume work entitled *American Entomology.* His huge collection of insects was, unfortunately, eaten by beetles after his death. At the utopian community of New Harmony, Indiana, Say met his wife, Lucy, who studied shells and would become the first woman elected to the Philadelphia Academy of Science.

**♪ Audubon tied a silver thread to the legs of young phoebes.**

In 1854 Audubon's eastern and Say's phoebes were renamed *Sayornis* (in honor of Say). The eastern phoebe is now *Sayornis phoebe,* and Say's phoebe is *S. saya.* The black phoebe is *S. nigricans.* The common name "phoebe," sometimes "phebe," is more likely an imitation of the bird's call than a connection with the Greek goddess.

# Pigeon or Dove

We think of foul sidewalks in connection with pigeons but peace and the Holy Spirit in connection with doves. These names are really interchangeable. "Pigeon" comes from *pipere*, Latin for "to cheep," and "dove" from *dubo*, the bird's Old German name. Their family, Columbidae, comes from the Latin for "pigeon or dove."

Charles Darwin bred exotic pigeons, painstakingly backcrossing them to obtain a pigeon identical to *Columba livia*, the rock dove, which he concluded was the ancestor of *all* our domestic pigeons. This dove from hilly Palestine was released by Noah to check the flood line and was also used sacrificially by the Jews. A dove spoke holy words into Muhammad's ear, although some say it was hungrily seeking a kernel of grain hidden there.

Their courtship "billing and cooing" is ardent and protracted, and doves, which are monogamous, symbolize love. Charles Bonaparte, Napoleon's nephew, named the American mourning dove after his wife, Zénaïde. The couple had twelve children. The "voice of the turtle," immortalized in the Song of Solomon, was that of the turtle dove, a migrant to the Holy Land whose return signaled spring and new love. But pigeons were also used in war: Julius Caesar sent pigeons back with news of his Gallic campaign; during the Crusades the Arabs used a pigeon post; more recently, in World War II, pigeons carried messages through enemy lines so successfully that some were given military decorations for their valor.

> **In World War II, pigeons carried messages through enemy lines so successfully that some were given military decorations for valor.**

The ancient sport of pigeon racing called *la guerra,* or "war game," was brought to New York by Italian immigrants. In a form of gang warfare flocks of pigeons were trained to return to a home roof at the sound of a horn, without being captured by the rival gang. Pigeons fly in close-knit flocks to confuse birds of prey, and a "stray pigeon" will sometimes join a flock for safety. The rival gang would try to capture, ransom, or kill its enemy's stray pigeon. This was also done by sewing shut the eyes of another pigeon and tying it to a stool (hence, "stool pigeon"), causing the stool pigeon to flap its wings, which is how pigeons attract one another. In this way, one gang would lure and kidnap its enemy's pigeon.

Along with horses and rats, pigeons have no gall bladder. Shakespeare (who evidently knew pigeons) has Hamlet say, "I am pigeon-liver'd, and lack gall." Pigeons also drink in a distinctive manner, immersing their heads and bills to suck up water, rather than tipping their heads back at each sip. Shakespeare's "sucking dove" may refer to pigeons feeding their nestlings "pigeon milk," a cheesy substance manufactured in the parents' crop lining. It is rich enough to support the young squabs (from the Swedish *skvabb,* "flabby") for the first few weeks of life.

American passenger pigeons were once so abundant it seemed impossible that hunting them and destroying their habitats could wipe them out completely. To early settlers the right to hunt freely was symbolically very important because in Europe only aristocrats kept pigeons, which could not be controlled even if they ravaged people's crops, and hunting privileges were reserved for the elite. This is why French revolutionaries wasted no time at all in abolishing *pigeonniers* (dovecotes) on August 26, 1789.

# PLOVER

The plover family is the Charadriidae, named after a mythical medieval bird called the Charadrius, or Caladrius. This bird could tell a sick man (always a man in the legend, never a woman!) whether he would live or die. If the Caladrius turned away from the patient, he would die. He would live if the Caladrius looked into his eyes and then flew up toward the sun, "burning up . . . his infirmity and dispersing it," claimed a medieval bestiary.

In spite of their family name, plovers don't always tally with descriptions of the Caladrius, and the Greek word *charadra,* from which the name comes, doesn't help us either. It means "ravine," but plovers are shorebirds that search for food on open meadows or beaches. However, plovers do have very large eyes and excellent eyesight, and even if their vision can't accurately prognosticate mortality, plovers are very good at spotting the little insects that they eat. They pluck up their prey with short straight bills, dashing after it in spurts.

The plover's common name comes from the Latin *pluvia,*

"rain," but, again, we don't know why. In 1555 the French naturalist Pierre Belon said the "pluvier" is "more easily caught during rainy weather." Their German name is *regenpfeifer,* or "rain piper," implying that the birds sing in the rain.

Lapwings, sometimes called "green plovers," are crested plovers with wattles. Though not native to North America, they are widespread elsewhere. Their scientific name, *Vanellus,* means "fan," probably given because of their rather slow, steady wing beat. They have white patches on their wings which appear to blink as they fly. The Old English name for lapwing was *lhapwynche,* from the Anglo-Saxon *hleape wince,* meaning "leaping from side to side." Plovers defend their young by running back and forth, pretending to be injured (dragging a wing). In this way they attract predators to themselves, distracting them from their chicks. If this strategy fails, lapwings also circle and cry loudly. They are also, in imitation of their cry, called peewits, or *wypes* (*vipa* in German). The noisy *Charadrius vociferus* cries "killdeer," and that is what we call it. The less paranoid dotterel allows humans to approach its nest, so earning the name of a "dote," or fool.

**Their eggs are conical at one end, so that they tend to roll back into the shallow nest if shifted.**

Plovers and lapwings nest in open places in scraped-out shallows, laying four "pyriform" eggs, which are conical at one end, so that they tend to roll back into the scrape if shifted.

These eggs are a gastronomic delicacy. In Britain the "Lapwing Act" of 1926 made taking lapwings' eggs illegal.

Because the eggs are so well camouflaged it is easy to approach the nest unintentionally. Modern birders worry about destroying nests, but Scottish Presbyterian Covenanters, plotting against the restoration of the Episcopalian Church in the seventeenth century, worried for another reason. If the fugitives stumbled on a lapwing nest while hiding on the moors, the bird would circle above them screaming, thus demonstrating to their pursuers exactly where the rebels could be caught. No wonder lapwings were considered "unlucky" birds in Scotland.

# PUFFIN

**M**ost of us would recognize a puffin. Its festive striped bill-covering (developed during the breeding season and then shed) is a prominent triangle, reminiscent of a carnival nose. Its wings are short, its tail stubby, and comically walking upright, it guarantees our bipedally anthropomorphic affection.

Nonetheless, the fat fledglings of puffins were often eaten, and a "puffin" meant a puffed-up, downy chick. John Caius, the founder of Caius College, Cambridge, kept a "puphin" in his room for eight months. Puffins nest in colonies on coastal cliffs or dig burrows in soil. Both parents feed the single chick until it is extremly fat. Before it is fully fledged the parents desert the chick, which, alone at night, leaves the nest for the sea. Puffins don't fly well, finding it hard to take off from the water, and use their short wings to help them dive and swim.

The puffin's scientific name isn't *Puffinus,* because that name was irrevocably given to two young shearwaters in 1678. Their scientific name, *Fratercula* (meaning "little brother"), is either because their head coloring is like a monk's cowl or because they clasp their feet together prayerfully when taking off. A nineteenth-century name for puffins was *mormon,* which was from the Greek *mormo,* "goblin," and had nothing to do with the Mormon religion. Puffins were also called "sea parrots" or, in parts of Britain, "coulter nebs." *Neb* is the ancient word for "bill," *coulter* the blade of a plow. The puffin's wedge-shaped bill is useful for holding a mouthful of fish.

**♆ A "puffin" means a puffed-up, downy chick.**

Puffins are in the Alcidae family (from the Icelandic *alka,* "auk"), which included the now extinct great auk (*see* Penguin). Other alcids include guillemots (from the French name for William) and dovekies. Most alcids have no hind toe, and some suggest the dovekie's scientific name, *Alle alle,* comes from the Latin *allex* ("big toe"), with the *x* dropped to show something is missing! Others say it's a Norse word.

When aboard a ship, John Audubon kept several puffins for about a week. He called them "agreeable pets only that they emitted an unpleasant grunting noise, and ran about incessantly during the night." He decided to throw them overboard, "where the water was beautifully clear" and, apparently without regret, described watching them dive down, and rapidly swim away.

# QUAIL

**T**he Israelites wandering in the wilderness with Moses were provided with water and manna, but, we are told, they "fell a-lusting . . . and said 'Who shall give us flesh to eat?'" It was then that they awoke to find quails "two cubits high" around their camp.

These would have been European common quails, *Coturnix coturnix* (Latin for "quail"), which in the autumn migrate in vast numbers from Europe to Africa. Actually, quails are better built for running than sustained flight (they have chunky bodies and short wings), and their migratory flight across the Mediterranean is about all they can manage. Pliny told that migrating quails rested in such numbers on the sails of ships at night that the vessels were in danger of sinking. No doubt the piles of birds found by the Hebrews were lying utterly exhausted after a particularly difficult flight.

The Israelites gathered quails "all that day and all that night and all the next day," and stuffed themselves with meat. But it seems it was more than mere overeating that made the Hebrews sick, because they were soon so ill many of them died, and the survivors felt thoroughly chastised for their greed by "the wrath of the Lord." In fact these quails were probably poisonous, because after crossing the Mediterranean, starved and dehydrated, quails sometimes land on the coast of Africa and fill up on plants that *they* can tolerate but cause their flesh to become poisonous. As Aristotle warned, "Some fruits are unfit for us to eat, but fit for others, like the henbane and hellebore, which are poisonous to men, but good food for quails."

> 𝒜 A seventeenth-century naturalist wrote that quails when mating were "infamous for obscene and unnatural lust."

French cookbooks are lyrical in praise of the quail's tender white breasts. Because they avoid flying, quails provide plenty of white meat. Strong-flying game birds are more likely to develop dark meat from the rich blood supply to their well-worked muscles. The old Dutch *quacken,* "to croak," Latinized to *quacula* in the eighth century, forms the root of the quail's French name, *caille,* and our name for them too, even though they don't really quack like ducks.

Perhaps because they are associated with delicious eating, quails are also connected with the intimacy that often follows a good meal. A sixteenth-century writer suggested that husband and wife should each wear a quail's heart (perhaps after they had consumed the rest of the body), "the husband that of the male, the wife that of the female," to promote marital bliss. But the seventeenth-century English naturalist John Ray considered mating quails "infamous for obscene and unnatural lust." Anyway, the word "quail" often meant a prostitute and, according to the Oxford English Dictionary, a "bevy" is a "company of ladies, roes, quails or larks," which is certainly not a humdrum collection, whatever way you would wish to interpret it.

# RAVEN

Ravens are big, comely birds with beautiful glossy black plumage, and ever since the Song of Songs, for Solomon's beloved, dark-haired lovers have had "raven tresses." But for some their blackness had another side: In early legends ravens were thought to have sinned and, as punishment, been changed by the gods from white to black. Because they are scavengers, following weak animals and waiting for them to die, ravens were also associated with the darkness of death. A "ravenstone" meant a place of execution, and "an unkindness of ravens" is the ominous name for a group of ravens.

Although omnivorous, ravens prefer to eat meat, but their bills, which look so formidable, are not strong enough to penetrate the hide (or clothes) of corpses. For that they must either rely on other animals or get at the meat by piercing through the eyes of the carcass. The traditional association of ravens with hunters (depicted in the cave drawings at Lascaux) may be because these birds followed hunters, who were apt to leave accessible meat. Ravens hide surplus food in caches, and the prophet Elijah, whom God "commanded the ravens to feed," perhaps followed the birds to their hiding places.

The raven's scientific name, *Corvus corax,* is from the Greek *korax,* a "croaker," reflecting its guttural cry, and these birds are in the Corvidae, or crow family. The common name "raven" comes from the Old Norse word *hrafn,* meaning to clear one's throat. Spoken aloud, *hrafn* reminds us that even

**♀ "Raven's knowledge" means an acquaintance with the supernatural.**

back in the dimmest past there must have been plenty of phlegmy throats and rheumy eyes. The name somewhat lost its vividness when the *h* was no longer sounded, and when it was dropped, the bird became a "raven."

Perhaps because they could mimic human speech, ravens were considered messengers and prophets. "Raven's knowledge" means an acquaintance with the supernatural. The Norse god Odin was accompanied by two ravens, Hugin (his thought) and Munin (his memory). Charles II kept ravens in the Tower of London because a soothsayer had told him disaster would befall the nation if they left, and ravens have been there ever since. They were often kept as pets. Charles Dickens put his pet raven, called Grip, into his novel *Barnaby Rudge,* where it repeatedly said, "I'm a Devil."

Like humans, ravens are sociable and usually mate for life,

both habits (strangely enough) considered characteristics of intelligent creatures. Ravens have brains that are large in proportion to their body size. They can also count quite well. In spite of this, Edgar Allan Poe's famous raven replied to the poet's agonized questioning about the meaning of life with little perception. And the raven's answer "Nevermore" is "nothing more" than a rhyme for the beloved's name, "Lenore," as well as the "shore" where the poet did "implore." It seems that the bird, lacking any real intuition, was merely repeating the sounds it heard. It's easy to read much into the remarkable abilities of ravens, but their talents are for their own uses, not ours.

# RHEA

Rhea was the wife of Cronus, or Saturn. Cronus, fearing a prophesy that one of his children would supplant him, ate his offspring as soon as each was born. Rhea, desperate to save her son Zeus, gave birth in a remote cave and, leaving the baby with her mother, came home with a stone wrapped in swaddling clothes, which Cronus gulped down without even inspecting. Actually, although rheas do swallow stones, it is the *females* who don't take much notice of their babies, heading out right after depositing an egg in a communal nest and leaving the male to incubate and raise the chicks alone. But Linnaeus probably didn't know that when he gave these South American birds the name *Rhea americana*.

In 1833, Charles Darwin left the *Beagle* to travel by land across

Patagonia, where he saw rheas, which, he said, "present a very noble appearance." The specimen he sent home to the London Zoological Society turned out to be different from *R. americana,* or the greater rhea, and was called Darwin's rhea in his honor. Its scientific name is *Pterocnemia pennata,* from the Greek *pteron,* "feather," and *kneme,* "shin," because these rheas have feathers covering part of their legs. *Pennata* means "winged," although rheas can't fly.

**The Greek goddess Rhea was the wife of Cronus, who ate his children as soon as they were born.**

Rheas are exclusively South American birds, but they look a bit like ostriches, which live in Africa. Like ostriches, rheas eat stones to aid their digestion (they have no crop). Distinctions between them include the rhea's three toes, instead of the ostrich's two. Rheas stretch their necks horizontally in front of them when they run, but ostriches hold their heads upright. Rheas lift one wing when turning, and their wings cover their rumps like a cloak. They have no handsome ostrich plumes, and their feathers are not much used commercially, except as dusters. Ostriches live in dry deserts, but rheas like to be near water and swim very well. The male rhea's cry is a deep roar, which Darwin thought was like the sound "made by a wild beast."

In spite of these differences, experts in avian parasitism discovered that ostriches and rheas are both hosts of the same two parasites, a feather louse and a tapeworm. It's unlikely that these two parasites could have traveled across the world any time recently, to find these particular two birds separately. It looks as if the rheas and the ostriches might have shared a common ancestor that harbored these parasites, so long ago that the continents were not yet divided. So perhaps Darwin, who thought rheas were "another species of ostrich," wasn't *quite* so wrong.

# ROADRUNNER

The roadrunner, as well as being a cartoon character, is a type of cuckoo. Less surprisingly, roadrunners avoid flying, preferring to run (along roads!). They can reach speeds of fifteen miles an hour.

Roadrunners were not classified in Europe until the nineteenth century, when they were named by Johann Wagler, who was best known for his work on snakes. Roadrunners themselves fiercely attack snakes, sometimes draping them around their bills to carry back to their young. They also hunt toads and lizards, as well as insects and small mammals. Before swallowing their prey, they batter it against a hard surface to break all the bones, reducing it to a mushy pulp. Unlike some birds, roadrunners don't have to regurgitate bones, feathers, or fur but digest the lot. They lose heat at night (when they can't hunt anyway), and most of their victims are cold-blooded, meaning they are also inactive at night. In the morning, before beginning to look for food, the birds sunbathe to regain their body temperature, helped by the heat-absorbent dark skin and feathers on their backs.

The roadrunner's scientific name is *Geococcyx,* meaning "ground cuckoo." There are two species: *Geococcyx californianus* (of California) is the greater roadrunner, and *G. velox* (fast) is the lesser roadrunner, which is found in Mexico and Central America. One of their common names, "chaparral cock," comes from the Spanish *chaparra,* or "evergreen oak," which grows in scrubby deserts where the birds live. In Mexico the roadrunner is called *paisano,* or "compatriot," and they can be tamed quite easily.

**In Mexico the roadrunner is called *paisano,* or "compatriot," and they can be tamed quite easily.**

Roadrunners are about two feet in length, with long tails and zygodactyl feet, like other cuckoos. This means that two toes point forward and two back, making it hard to tell from their tracks whether they were going forward or backward. Pueblo Indians used to surround the houses of their dead with a scratched pattern of roadrunner tracks, to confuse any evil spirits that might be lurking around.

# ROBIN

In John Woolman's famous Quaker *Journal* he confesses that as a boy he stoned a mother robin. He then climbed to the nest and killed the fledglings, "supposing that better than to leave them to pine away and die miserably." He was "much troubled," and his religious life began. Although the event was important to the history of Quakerism, he need not have killed the nestlings. The male robin frequently takes over their feeding while the female leaves to start another brood.

Woolman, who was born in 1720 and grew up in New Jersey, was writing about American robins, which were misnamed by early settlers. Both the American and European robins have red breasts, but the European robin, *Erithacus rubecula* (from the Greek *erithakos,* "solitary," and the Latin for "little red one"), is not a true thrush. Unlike American robins, European robins never congregate in flocks. American robins are large thrushes, named *Turdus migratorius* by Linnaeus, from the Latin *turdus,* "thrush," and because they migrate in winter. Their French name was *le merle d'Amérique.* The European blackbird, *T. merula,* is much more nearly related to American robins than is their namesake.

But robins on both sides of the Atlantic are thought of as friends to humans, and the name "robin" was a diminutive of the Norman name "Robert." Robins look for grubs in loose soil, often waiting for gardeners to turn it over for them. Their tameness around people was long interpreted as reciprocal affection, and in European legend their red breast was said to have been scorched in hell when they brought us the gift of fire, or else was from blood, when the robin gallantly plucked at Christ's crown of thorns. It is easy for us to dismiss John Webster's belief that robins "with leaves and flow'rs do cover / The friendless bodies of unburied men," but our forefathers, greatly fearing unhallowed death in lonely forests, were comforted by the idea, which may have come from seeing robins shifting woody debris to find food.

> **Their red breast was said to have been scorched in hell when these birds brought us the gift of fire.**

Robins flourished noticeably in America as land was cultivated, because of a new and better food for them: the earthworm. Settlers unwittingly reintroduced what we think of as "ordinary" garden worms. These immigrant Lumbricidae worms had been eliminated during the ice age in North America, but when they increased again robins increased too. Small wonder, for one study shows that a baby robin can ingest *fourteen feet* of earthworms in one day!

David Lack's famous study of English robins (begun in 1935) showed that males spend much of their lives fighting, never sitting sweetly side by side, as pictured on Christmas cards. They are stimulated by the color of their rival's breast, and robins even attacked a tuft of red breast feathers detached by Lack from its defunct original owner. In one of Wordsworth's poems the unbrotherly robin that saddened the poet when it "chased a butterfly" was probably stimulated by the butterfly's "crimson as bright as thine own."

We want robins to behave as we think friends should. And as they tunefully ward off rivals from their nesting territory, *we* insist they are "joyfully" announcing to us that spring has arrived.

# SANDPIPER

We love to watch sandpipers nipping along borders of glistening foam, darting for food and "piping" through the sound of the waves. Several species frequently gather in the same place, the varying length of their bills and their preferred prey allowing them to feed alongside one another. These little earth-colored birds, which dash up and down beaches searching for food, live on the edges of the water all over the world, and range in size from five inches to two feet long.

Sandpipers are often called "shorebirds" in America and "waders" in Britain. Many of them have the genus name *Tringa* or *Calidris,* both of which simply mean "sandpiper" in Greek. But not all sandpiper names stop there. One sandpiper, the red knot, was given its scientific name, *Calidris canutis,* by Linnaeus. This bird, called "Canute's Bird of Old" by Michael Drayton, the poet who died in 1631, was traditionally connected with the eleventh-century Danish king Canute the Great. Canute exposed the shameless flattery of his courtiers. To emphasize that he was not omnipotent, as the obsequious insisted, the king ordered the tide to go back, but unimpressed by his royal power, the waves continued to rise. Knots often feed at the edge of surf, waiting for the waves to retreat, then probing with their long bills into the exposed sand. This nice association, however, is somewhat spoiled by sober etymologists, who, preferring scholarship to romance, tell us it is "baseless." The name "knot" or a "knotty" was first used in 1452, supposedly in imitation of the bird's "grunting call," but possibly something to do with gnats—an etymological link offered here for what, if anything, it is worth.

**Sandpipers live on the edges of water all over the world.**

Other sandpipers include the dunlin, the sanderling, the godwit, the willet and the dowitcher. The poetry of these names is more in their music than their meaning: dunlin means "dun-colored"; sanderling is the bird's Icelandic name; godwit means a "good bird" (to eat); willet imitates its call; dowitcher comes either from *Deutschers* or *Duitsch,* because German and Dutch Americans liked to eat them, or is their Indian name. Dowitchers scurry along the sand, jabbing with their bills in what is called a "sewing machine" motion.

Sandpipers don't swim much, but they fly well. They migrate long distances, sometimes from one end of the earth to the other. Before migrating, they must accumulate enough fat to sustain them for the journey, and they feed in flocks on beaches.

*Sandpiper*

When we innocently interrupt this serious business by walking along the beach (even to admire them), they stop feeding and fly up at our approach. If they don't have a chance to store enough fat for their trip, they won't be back next year, or ever, for us to watch, even from a distance.

# SAPSUCKER

Sapsuckers feed by drilling lines of vertical or horizontal holes through the bark of trees, then using the brushlike tips of their tongues to soak up the oozing sap. They also eat insects attracted to the syrup, and some of the soft bark too.

This is not very good for the tree, although the birds often move to a new one before it is fatally damaged. But in the days when home owners grew apples more than they watched birds, Neltje Blanchan, usually ecstatic about our "Bird Neighbors," in her 1904 book of that name described the sapsucker taking the "heart-blood" of fruit trees. It was, she wrote, "one of the few bird visitors whose intimacy should be discouraged."

The sapsucker's name, *Sphyrapicus,* is from the Greek *sphyra,* "hammer," and the Latin *picus* (*see* Woodpecker). The male Williamson's sapsucker is unique among American sapsuckers because the male has no red on top of its head (although it has a red chin). The females, who migrate farther south than the males, look very different, and for a long time the two sexes were thought to be different species. In the early 1850s John Cassin, working at the Natural Academy of Sciences in Philadelphia, named the bird *Sphyrapicus thyroideus,* for a female specimen he received. The bird had a shieldlike black patch on her chest, and the Greek *thyreos* means "shield," and *eidos,* "like."

Males of the same species were found in 1857 by the naturalist Dr. John Newberry, who thought them to be a different bird. Newberry called his bird *S. williamsoni,* in honor of Lieutenant Robert Stockton Williamson, the leader of a government survey to explore a railway route between San Francisco and Oregon. Newberry had

**For a long time the two sexes of Williamson's sapsucker were thought to be different species.**

been sent by the Smithsonian Institution to accompany the expedition, a custom instigated so that naturalists would be protected by government troops. It also saved the Smithsonian money. Williamson became so sick he had to be sent back to San Francisco, but Newberry named the bird for him anyway.

In 1873, however, Henry Henshaw noticed that an *S. williamsoni* was nesting with what he had thought was another species, *S. thyroideus,* and he "saw proof positive of their relationship"! After that, both male and female became *S. thyroideus,* sharing the common name "Williamson's."

Henshaw, who had discovered this by observation in the field, wrote disparagingly that "it is difficult to understand why the true facts of the case should so long have escaped the notice of closet naturalists." By Henshaw's time it was not enough for ornithologists to examine skins and sort species—they were expected, as they still are today, to go out themselves and *watch* birds.

# Secretary Bird

When secretary birds were named they looked like the secretaries of the day. They have a spray of feathers projecting from the back of their heads, reminiscent of old-time secretaries, who stuck spare quill pens behind their ears or in their hair. Quill pens were used from the sixth century B.C. until a little over a hundred years ago. The hollow shaft of large feathers, developed by birds for strength and lightness, held ink, and the unique flexibility of these feathers allowed the ink to be released gradually when a small slit (cut with a "penknife") was opened slightly by the writer's pressure. When they were first tried, no metal nibs could be made that controlled a gradual flow of ink like flexible feather quills. No one produced a usable nib until, in 1830, a man called James Perry patented the idea of cutting a hole in the center of the slit in a metal nib, making the point flexible, and metal pens replaced quills. Quill pens, however, are still the preferred tools of some artists, and they are made only from certain feathers of certain large birds, including swans, geese, and crows (but not secretary birds).

The secretary bird is the only member of its family, Sagittari- idae, because although it is similar to several other birds, it doesn't fit into any of their families: It flies and soars as well as an eagle; it is over three feet tall and runs like an ostrich; it nests like a stork; some of its face is bare, like a vulture's; it partly digests and regurgitates food for its young; and it's a raptor.

*They have a spray of feathers reminiscent of old-time secretaries, who stuck spare quill pens behind their ears.*

The secretary bird has short stubby toes, which it can't use to carry prey but with which it literally stomps its victims to death. It has such a powerful kick that it can shatter a turtle's shell, and it kills snakes by kicking or dropping them from a height. Its scientific name, *Sagittarius serpentarius,* means "a bowman hunting snakes," and the bird's head plumes are also like arrows sticking out of a quiver. Most bow hunters, though, would hunt more sportingly!

# SHRIKE

William Turner, in a *Short and Succint History of Birds* (1544), called the red-backed shrike "a nyn murder" because the bird was believed to murder and collect nine victims a day. Its German name was *Nuenmörder,* now *Neuntöter.* The name "shrike" comes from "shriek," describing the bird's alarm call, although these birds also sing sweetly and can mimic other birds.

Shrikes are the only passerines that prey on vertebrate animals, often impaling the carcasses on thorns to store for future use. This habit gave them the family name Laniidae, from the Latin *lanius,* "a butcher." They are sometimes called butcher birds in English. The common French name for the red-backed shrike was once *l'écorcheur,* or "flayer," from the bird's habit of tearing apart or skinning small mammals before eating them.

The two shrikes found in North America are the loggerhead shrike, *Lanius ludovicianus* ("from Louisiana"), and the northern shrike, *L. excubitor.* The loggerhead shrike gets its common name from its head, which, as in all shrikes, is squarish and large in proportion to its body, accommodating its strong jaw muscles. Shrikes use only their sturdy bills, not their feet, to kill and carry their prey. The northern shrike, also called the great gray shrike, lives and breeds in northern areas of the Old and the New Worlds. The *excubitor* part of its name means "watchman." Linnaeus explained that he gave the bird this name because it "observat et aviculis indicat," which is usually translated as "looks out for [hawks] and warns little birds." This protective gesture puzzles ornithologists, because shrikes hunt and eat small birds. Perhaps Linnaeus meant that the shrike inadvertently "alerts" rather than "warns" little birds with the shrill scream it emits whenever it spots a hawk.

**They are sometimes called butcher birds.**

In December 1850, Henry David Thoreau watched a shrike pecking a small bird to pieces and commented, "I had not associated such actions with my idea of birds. It was not bird-like." The shrike's larder of corpses stuck on branches is certainly not a bucolically reassuring sight. But apart from storing surplus food, leaving it to "hang" can, as shrikes have discovered, neutralize the poisons in creatures such as insects and frogs, which might otherwise be inedible. We humans prefer to keep meat hooks and carcasses out of public sight, purchasing our own "prey" in soothing Styrofoam trays, covered with plastic.

# Skimmer

Skimmers skim over the water surface to feed, rarely wetting their bodies. They fly back and forth across the calm water, cutting into it with their lower bill until they hit prey, at which instant the upper bill snaps down, and their heads bend underneath their bodies to take the impact. They have unique bills. The lower mandible, which is like a sharp flat knife, is much longer than the upper, which is narrow and oval. The eighteenth-century naturalist Mark Catesby called the bird a "cutwater," but the name did not endure. Skimmers are sometimes called "scissorbills," or *bec à ciseaux* in French.

**Throughout the bird's life the lower bill grows twice as fast as the upper, to replace the wear on it from friction.**

They often feed in shallow estuaries at high tide and are sometimes called "flood gulls." Skimmers can see in the dark, feeding at night as well as day, and are the only birds with *vertically* slit pupils (like a cat's) that close in bright light.

Their subfamily name, Rynchopinae, from the Greek *rhunkhos,* "bill," and *ops,* "face," refers to their peculiar bills. Young skimmers, though, have mandibles of equal length and can pick up food from the ground, but as they learn to skim, the lower bill lengthens. Throughout the bird's life the lower bill grows twice as fast as the upper, to replace the wear on it from friction. A skimmer's bill, wrote Catesby, is "a wonderful work of nature." Indeed it is.

# Skua

Skuas, which are very large gulls, are brigands and scavengers. They attack other birds, forcing them to relinquish their catch; they raid nests, devouring eggs and fledglings; and they chase other creatures from beached carcasses. The great skua, about two feet long, can catch and eat quite large mammals.

The name "skua" comes from the Faeroe Islands, where the bird was called a *skuvur* and is still called a *skooie*. Another name that comes from Norn (the language once spoken in the Faeroes and Shetlands) is Bonxie, from *bunke,* a "fat woman."

Skuas are Larids (gulls). They eat offal, and the name of their genus, Stercorarius, means "of dung." Large southern skuas are sometimes called *Catharacta* (from the Greek *kathartes,* "a cleanser"), because they clean up beaches. In America (but not in Britain) some skuas are called jaegers, from the German *Jäger,* or "hunter," which has the same root as "yacht" (once the word for a fast pirate ship). Some older books give jaegers the family name Lestridinae, from the Greek *leistris,* "pirate."

Skuas and jaegers have a saddlelike bridge, or "cere," across the top of their upper bill. The pomarine jaeger gets its name from the Greek *poma,* "covering," and *rhis,* "nose." *Catharacta maccormicki* was named for Dr. Robert McCormick, who traveled to the Arctic and Antarctic. The doctor was with Captain James Ross when he took Possession Island in 1841. During the rapid conquest of this small island, celebrated by drinking champagne toasts to Queen Victoria and raising the British flag, McCormick shot the skua that bears his name. We are told that possessing the island and acquiring the bird took the company all of twenty-five minutes! This skua is the only bird named for McCormick, who was considered by his contemporaries to be a poor naturalist, more interested in shooting birds than classifying them. Until he asked to be sent home, McCormick was on the *Beagle* with Charles Darwin, who wrote, "My friend the Doctor is an ass, but we jog on very amicably." In his last years McCormick was ignored by the scientific world and apparently took solace in a pet house sparrow, which shared his meals with him until he died.

**2. The name "skua" comes from the Faeroe Islands.**

# SNAKEBIRD

S nakebirds have very long sinuous necks and often swim half-submerged, with their heads and necks protruding serpentlike out of the water. Indeed, to the first Europeans who caught sight of snakebirds swimming, they looked more like water serpents than birds: "In those countries where noxious animals abound, we may readily conceive that the appearance of this bird . . . would tend to startle the wary traveller," wrote Alexander Wilson.

The American snakebird, or anhinga, lives in tropical swamps and bayous from the Gulf states to Argentina, always feeding in fresh water. The name "anhinga" is from the Tupi in Brazil, meaning a devil bird or evil spirit. This bird was first described by a German naturalist, Georg Marcgraf, who escaped from the Thirty Years War to explore Brazil. He died of fever in 1644 (aged only thirty-three). His notes were collected, and Linnaeus used them to name the bird *Anhinga plotinus* (from the Greek *plotos,* "floating"). The name was later changed to *A. anhinga*.

Outside America members of the Anhingidae family are called darters, because of their pointed bills, which they use to spear fish. The Anhingidae have a unique spinal formation. The eighth vertebra of their S-shaped neck is fused almost horizontally, forming a hinge, allowing the birds to thrust their heads rapidly forward.

**♫ Early explorers at first thought these extraordinary birds might be monstrous crosses between ducks and snakes.**

Like cormorants, their nearest relatives, anhingas dive from the water surface, not from the air, and they have to spread their wings to dry them. In some ways anhingas look a bit like very slender cormorants, but not in others. Anhingas can fan out their tails like turkeys, and in North America they are sometimes called water turkeys. In parts of Florida, the anhinga was once called a "Grecian lady" because of its graceful curving neck. Its Creole name, *bec à lancette,* means "sharp bill."

Early explorers to America at first thought these extraordinary birds might be monstrous crosses between ducks and snakes. William Bartram described the anhinga in this way: "I doubt not but if this bird had been an inhabitant of the Tiber in Ovid's days, it would have furnished him with a subject, for some beautiful and entertaining metamorphoses."

# SPARROW

It isn't surprising to discover that in ancient times *passer,* the Latin word for "sparrow," meant any small fluttering bird, for we too refer to many little brown birds, not necessarily related, as sparrows. The name "sparrow" comes from the Old English *spearw,* meaning "a flutterer." The French name is *moineau,* from *moine,* a monk, because of sparrows' drab, cowl-like plumage, and the British hedge sparrow is called a "dunnock" or "little dun bird," for the same reason.

The ubiquitous house sparrow, *Passer domesticus* ("domesticated"), originated in India and the Mediterranean, spreading with civilization and flourishing where they could feed from the droppings of cattle and horses. By the time of Jesus, these sparrows were so abundant in Palestine that the disciples were told that two could be bought "for one farthing," or five for "two farthings" (allowing an "extra" bird to be thrown into the bargain). But each sparrow was counted by God, just as, said Jesus, "the very hairs of your head are numbered."

Not only God but ornithologists too count hairs—or feathers. In 1935 Alexander Wetmore published *The Number of Feathers in the English Sparrow,* which reported that, not including the downy underfeathers, the number varied seasonally, from 1,359 to 3,352. Far from being irrelevant, the number of a "sparrow's" feathers can have taxonomic importance. Most of the New World birds we call "sparrows" have nine primary wing feathers and belong to the Emberizidae family (*see* Bunting). They are not related to Eurasian sparrows, which have ten primary wing feathers and are in the Passeridae family.

**2 The name "sparrow" comes from the Old English *spearw,* meaning "a flutterer."**

Some Old World sparrows, however, were introduced to America and elsewhere, thriving so well they now seem like natives. The most notable is the house sparrow, sometimes (inaccurately) called the English sparrow. It was introduced to North America in the nineteenth century, and in 1871 Marianne North, a Victorian lady traveler and artist, wrote, "In and about all the great towns of the States I saw little houses built for the accommodation of sparrows; the birds had been imported from England to get rid of a caterpillar. . . . The sparrows seemed to take kindly to their new homes and diet, but it was still a problem how they would endure the winter."

Not only did they endure, they multiplied, soon becoming pests, and Americans were divided as to whether they should be exterminated. Ornithologists on each side heatedly attacked one another, and the vituperative public argument became known as the "Sparrow War." But the sparrows were here to stay. Even though, in 1899, the American Ornithologists Union rejected the "eligibility" of the house sparrow to be an "American" bird, it finally had to be added to the checklist in 1931. The number of house sparrows decreased somewhat when horses were replaced by automobiles, but this immigrant is now one of our most ubiquitous birds.

The Venerable Bede compared the human soul to a little "sparrow," flitting through a hall: "It enters in at one door and quickly flies out through the other. . . . So this life of man appears but for a moment; what follows or indeed what went before, we know not at all."

# STARLING

A group of starlings is called a "murmuration," presumably because of their mingled chatter when they roost in thousands. Then they take off again, turning in unison through the skies, like one huge bird or millions of twirling stars. The starling's Anglo-Saxon name was *staer*. The "ing" suffix, a diminutive, was added later to form "starling." Some etymologists connect the name with a celestial star: In winter starlings have a speckled, or "starry," plumage, later replaced by glossy black; and when they fly they look a bit "star-shaped" from beneath. "Sterling" silver could, it is thought, also be connected with starlings, from Edward the Confessor's silver coins, which were marked with four birds.

*Sturnus* was the Latin name for "starling," and Pliny the Elder said he knew of a starling that talked in both Latin and Greek. Starlings (and their nearest relatives, mynah birds), are excellent mimics. In May 1784 Mozart bought his pet starling when he heard it in a shop, whistling the Allegretto from his G major concerto. More probably the composer had been whistling to himself and the bird had imitated him. When the starling died, three years later, Mozart buried it in his garden and wrote a sad epitaph. Mynahs are often kept as talking pets too, and the mynah's common name comes from the Hindi *maina,* a term of endearment, best translated as "pet."

**♪ Mozart bought his pet starling when he heard it in a shop, whistling the Allegretto from his G major concerto.**

Both starlings and mynahs seem to have been revered by the ancients. John Aubrey, a seventeenth-century English historian, called starlings "Druids' birds." He thought holes in the constructions at Stonehenge were left by the Druids "purposely for their Birds to nest in." Hindus encouraged mynahs to nest in their temples too.

Starlings originated in Asia, and there were none in the New World until humans introduced them. The common starling, *Sturnus vulgaris,* was deliberately brought to New York in 1890, when the American Acclimatization Society, led by Eugene Schieffelin, let loose forty pairs in Central Park. It is said that Schieffelin, who was also president of the Brooklyn Bird Club, was planning to bring all of Shakespeare's birds and flowers to America (although Shakespeare mentioned the starling only once, in *Henry IV*). More likely Schieffelin's group was hoping that starlings would destroy insect pests. But the birds increased rapidly, eating more grain and fruit than insects and becoming pests themselves. The introduction of mynahs to Hawaii to control cutworms on sugarcane also proved a misjudgment, threatening to outnumber native bird populations there.

In the Old World, as well, starlings often multiply alarmingly. They flourish in open agricultural land and in cities too, where they can nest on buildings. There were so many in London that on August 12, 1949, starlings perching on the hands of Big Ben stopped the famous clock. The British Parliament immediately met to consider ways of exterminating these birds, who had dared to threaten the sacred timepiece.

# STORK

Storks nest high, on treetops in the wild or on the roofs of houses. After migrating, they return to their huge nests year after year. Long ago, when a new baby was often an annual event, the reliable stork on the roof could conveniently explain where the child came from. Today storks still feature prominently on birth announcements.

Most people liked to have storks around because they eat frogs, snakes, locusts, and mice. Storks were believed to take care of their aging parents, so our ancestors also thought them good examples of filial duty. In some countries the penalty for killing a stork was death, and the Jews were always forbidden to eat them. Even so, some people made their own rules: In 1534 Henry VIII served a banquet of stork to his Lords of the Star Chamber. The legendary European white stork is *Ciconia ciconia,* from the Latin for "stork." The bird's Old English name was *storc,* which also meant "stick." This could be a reference to its habit of standing on one sticklike leg, or it could be an elaboration of the Old German dialect *Storch,* meaning "penis." The latter postulation would fit nicely with the stork's connection to human babies. An old Scottish word "storken" means "to become stiff."

But even if storks were believed to be responsible baby couriers, they are not, by our standards, trustworthy with their own young. They practice what ornithologists poetically term "chronism." Cronus, or Saturn, fearing that his children would supplant him, swallowed them as they were born (*see* Rhea). Storks will sometimes kill and eat some of their young, most probably because they cannot find enough food for them. They have about four to start with, in those lofty nests, and the young storks appropriately develop their wings very early and their long legs much later.

**⚕ In some countries the penalty for killing a stork was death.**

There are only a few storks in the New World, but the wood stork (sometimes called a wood ibis) can be found in the southern United States. Its name, *Mycteria americana,* is from the Greek *mukter,* "snout," presumably because of its long beak. Adults have a dark, bald pate and are sometimes called "flintheads." The voice box, or syrinx, of storks never completely develops, and they can only hiss or whistle. They communicate by clattering their bills. In his *Inferno* Dante described traitors wedged in the ice, their teeth chattering, "like the sound made by storks."

# SWALLOW

In a touching thirteenth-century legend, the Christ child plays in the mud, forming little birds, which come to life—and are swallows. This story reflected a belief that when swallows disappeared during the winter, they were hibernating in the mud at the bottom of ponds, to be resurrected in spring. Swallows do live near water and use mud to build their nests. Ornithologists did not agree that swallows migrate in winter until the end of the nineteenth century. In 1899, Dr. Benjamin Smith Barton, a respected naturalist, did not find it superfluous to state that "all my enquiries convince me, that our swallows are migratory birds."

Swallows have a high, twittery cry and constantly move. They have exceptionally good eyesight, changing focus rapidly as they chase insects, which they pursue individually with a characteristic jerky flight. Their Mohegan name, *Pons-pau-cloo-moose,* meant "bird that never rests." In Europe they were once thought to cure the uncontrollable motions of epilepsy, and a seventeenth-century recipe called for "40 or 50" swallows put *alive* into a mortar and pounded to make a medicine that "comforteth the brain." It was thought that mother swallows applied flowers of the greater celandine, or *Chelidonium,* to the eyes of her nestlings, which are born blind. The Greek name for swallow was *chelodian,* which is still part of the name of many swallows. The celandine was believed to cure human eye ailments too.

**♫ They were once thought to cure the uncontrollable motions of epilepsy.**

The Romans called swallows *hirundo,* from which they get their family name, Hirundinidae. The barn swallow is *Hirundo rustica,* meaning "from the country." The common name "swallow" comes from the Anglo-Saxon *swalewe,* which in turn comes from the Old Norse *svala,* meaning "cleft stick," referring to the swallows' forked tail. A 1990 Swedish study showed female swallows have a strong preference for symmetry in the male's forked tail, which could indicate the healthy cell division desirable in a mate.

Many swallows are called martins. The American bank swallow is the same bird as the British sand martin. Its name, *Riparia riparia,* means "riverbank," and these birds nest in holes. The English word "martin" comes from the French name, which is a diminutive of Mars, the name of the Roman god of war. The purple martin is *Progne subis,* after the Greek Procne, who was the daughter of Pandion (*see* Nightingale). In one of the several Greek and Roman versions of this story, Procne was turned into a swallow because she murdered her son. (*Subis* was Pliny the Elder's name for the bird.)

Purple martins come to nest in the United States in spring. People often provide nesting boxes for them because they are thought to control mosquitoes. Actually martins are diurnal (day) feeders, and are usually roosting by the time most mosquitoes emerge. But even if the birds don't eat *all* the mosquitoes, the martin houses are often elaborately beautiful, and their inhabitants, flitting in and out of the doors, are very nice to have around.

# SWAN

**M**any swan legends include swan maidens who leave their feather coverings aside to swim unclothed. A watching human steals the garments and possesses the maiden until, by accident or intent, she resumes her dress and becomes a swan once more. When real swans molt they lose all their flying feathers, or remiges, at one time, so, like naked damsels, they can't get away. They stay in the water with their babies, which can't fly either.

In Britain all swans belonged to the crown unless otherwise marked. The molting season was the season of "swan-upping," when swans were captured and marked with their owner's *cygni notae,* or patterned nicks in their bills. The practice began in the Middle Ages, and the royal swankeeper still rounds up swans on the Thames River and reports how many there are to the queen. Male swans, called cobs, look just like the pens, or females.

The Latin word for "swan" is *cygnus,* which also gives us the name of baby swans, or cygnets. Cycnus, a Greek mythological figure, was turned into a swan when, desperately unhappy, he threw himself into a lake. Jupiter (Zeus) also turned himself into a swan to seduce Leda, who in due course hatched the twins Castor and Pollux.

The mute swan, or *Cygnus olor,* was semidomesticated in Europe, and the name *olor* also means "swan" in Latin. The old name "swanne" has the same word root as the Latin *sonus* ("sound"), but the mute swan only grunts or hisses, except in legend, when it was said to sing its "swan song" before it died. The introduced European mute swans have orange bills with a distinctive black knob at the base and are the most familiar swans in the United States.

Until 1697, when Willem de Vlaming, a Dutch navigator in Australia, captured seven black swans (which died on the voyage home), black swans existed only in images of the devil. They were later brought to Europe, where the Empress Josephine kept them at Malmaison, but they never became widespread. The Siberian Bewick's swan was named in recognition of Thomas Bewick of Newcastle, who wrote *A History of British Birds* in 1804. Bewick started his career painting murals of hunting scenes on the houses of his "rustic neighbours." These were "faithfully delineated," he wrote, "in their opinion as well as my own." He later became famous for his engraving technique. Bewick's swans have individually patterned beaks, different on every bird.

The swans that most excited settlers in America were the enormous trumpeter swans, named, wrote the explorer John Lawson in 1709, "because of the sort of Trompeting Noise they make." These swans were hunted mercilessly, and between 1820 and 1880 the Hudson Bay company sent 108,000 swan skins to the London market. By the 1930s there were less than a hundred trumpeter swans in North America. Today they are still rare.

**♃ Jupiter turned himself into a swan to seduce Leda.**

All swans are protected now, although they are sometimes accused of depleting crops and fisheries. Their characteristic long necks, huge size, and grace in the water (which is where they have to both land and take off) make them seem magical. This quality, real or imaginary, is mirrored not only in glassy lakes but in our art, literature, and music.

# SWIFT

Because they were once thought to be very fast swallows, swifts were previously called "swift swallows," but they aren't related to swallows at all, and their nearest relatives are hummingbirds. Swifts are in the order Apodiformes, from the Greek *a,* "without," and *pous,* "foot." The European common swift is *Apus apus.* Swifts do have feet, but very small and weak ones, and unlike swallows they are never seen perching on telegraph wires, because swifts can't perch.

Indeed, swifts can hardly take off from the ground at all. To collect nesting materials they grab floating feathers or loose twigs, which they glue onto high vertical surfaces with their own saliva. Some swifts make nests using *only* their own saliva, from glands that enlarge during the breeding season. It takes about a month to accumulate enough saliva for each nest. These are used to make bird's nest soup, a Chinese delicacy that French epicures (mistakenly using the French word for "swallow"), call *Consommé aux nids d'hirondelle.*

The swifts that build these saliva nests are known as swiftlets. The genus *Collocalia* gets its name from the Greek *kolla,* "glue," and *kalia,* "nest," although nests of the swiftlet *Aerodramus* ("air traveler") contain the highest proportion of saliva and are used most often in soup. In the seventeenth century, a Dutch surgeon in Djakarta, Jacob Bontius, described the lucrative business in bird nests. The Dutch government soon exploited its colonial privileges, monopolizing the right to trade nests.

*They swoop overhead in masses, in what the poet Ted Hughes described as a "lunatic limber screaming frenzy."*

Collecting them from high cave walls is dangerous, and so, like many scarce commodities, the nests are reputed to have aphrodisiac properties. The connection could also be because swifts have the unusual ability to copulate while airborne. Otherwise, said the clerical naturalist Gilbert White, the swift "would seldom find opportunity for amorous rites." Swifts can remain airborne for very long periods, and are thought able even to sleep in the air if necessary.

Actually, they almost always roost. They can cling to vertical surfaces with all four toes pointing forward and upward. The chimney swift originally roosted in hollow trees, but now (as its name implies) sometimes roosts in chimneys. During their fall migration the birds layer themselves by the thousands in hollow cavities, propped upright with their weight supported by their stiff tails. Their name, *Chaetura pelagica,* comes from the Greek *chaite,* meaning "bristle," and *oura,* meaning "tail," for the bristly end of their tail. *Pelagica* was Linnaeus's irrevocable mistake when, in 1758, he named the bird *pelagios* ("marine"), intending to call it *pelasgia,* for the Pelasgi (a nomadic Greek tribe). Swifts aren't marine birds but are migratory wanderers. In 1766 Linnaeus corrected the name, but his original name was restored, because even for the father of nomenclature the rules of nomenclature weren't bent.

Swifts have the uncanny quality of becoming completely torpid during bad weather. When insects are available again they swoop overhead in masses, etching the sky with curling black swirls, in what the poet Ted Hughes described as a "lunatic limber screaming frenzy."

# TANAGER

In 1893, Antonín Dvořák took his family for a holiday to Spillville, Iowa. After eight months in New York, "I heard again the singing of birds," he wrote. Every morning at five A.M. the Bohemian composer walked in the woods along a stream, listening to American birds, which, he thought, "have much brighter colours and sing differently" than European birds. He incorporated the song of the scarlet tanager, a bird not found in the Old World, into his American Quartet in F.

Most tanagers are not notable vocalists. Schuyler Mathews, in *Wild Birds and Their Music* (1904), wrote that the scarlet tanager's voice is "a lazy drowsy, dozy buzz . . . which one can only liken to a giant musical bumblebee or an old-time hurdy gurdy." Others have described this bird's song as like that of a robin with a sore throat. It seems that Dvořák's stringed instruments were appropriate to portray it.

Tanagers are better known for their often very bright

plumage. They mostly live in the South American tropics, but four can be found in North America, where they come to breed in summer. The most common of these is the scarlet tanager, so called for the male's bright red nuptial plumage. The name "tanager" is a Brazilian Tupi name. Their scientific name is *Piranga olivacea*. *Piranga* is another South American name for the bird. Scarlet tanagers don't breed in South America, where the plumage of both males and females is olive and yellow *(olivacea)* and where they are *never* scarlet.

> 𝄞 **Dvořák incorporated the song of the scarlet tanager into his American Quartet in F.**

The other three tanagers which come to North America are the hepatic tanager, whose name comes from its color ("hepatic" means "liverish" or "jaundiced"), the summer tanager, and the western tanager, *P. ludoviciana,* named for the Louisiana Territory, where Lewis and Clark found it, sending the "frail remains" of the first specimen back to Philadelphia.

Scarlet tanagers visited Walden Pond, where Henry David Thoreau watched and heard them too. The tanager, he thought, "most takes the eye of any bird." When the "bloody fellow" flies through green trees, it seems "as if it would ignite the leaves." But Thoreau evidently did not share Dvořák's appreciation of the tanager's song: "With his harsh note," he wrote firmly, the tanager "pays for his color."

# THRUSH

Thrushes are frequently noted for their singing, and from Roman times were caged as songbirds. Giovanni Molina, who explored Chile in 1782, wrote that "it is not in the power of language to convey an idea of the song of the *thenca* [thrush]." But that hasn't prevented poets from trying. Thomas Hardy described a thrush singing of "Hope whereof he knew / And I was unaware." More optimistically, George Meredith said that a "Thrush in February" sings of "the young time with life ahead."

The thrush family, Turdidae, is a very large one and includes the seemingly unlikely but common members the American robin and the English blackbird. *Turdus* was the Romans' name for thrush, now its scientific name. The Middle English name was *thrusche,* from Anglo-Saxon *thryce.* For a long time the name "throstle" was more commonly used, as in Shakespeare's "throstle with his note so true." Another old name for the thrush was the "mavis," from its French name *mauvis*. In Scotland song thrushes are called "mavie throstles."

The European song thrush is *Turdus philomelos,* for its sweet song, like that of the nightingale, which was often called Philomel (*see* Nightingale). The mistle, or missel, thrush, which sings less sweetly, is *T. viscivorus* ("sticky"), for its supposed diet of sticky mistletoe berries. According to Thomas Pennant (the recipient of Gilbert White's famous eighteenth-century letters), "the misseltoe could not be propagated but by the berries that had passed through the body of this bird." Thrushes also eat insects and have very strong legs, with a "booted tarsus" (unscaled covering), which they use to scratch for food. Some thrushes have learned to get at snails by banging them against a stone to break the shell.

🎵 **Walt Whitman immortalized the bird in "When Lilacs Last in the Dooryard Bloom'd."**

The thrush's song comes from the syrinx, placed (lower down than our voice box) where the trachea divides to join the two bronchial tubes. Two membranes covering these openings can be tightened or loosened with a special set of muscles while air pressure from the lungs is altered. Not all birds that have these attributes use them to sing, but all virtuoso bird singers have them.

The American hermit thrush, *Catharus guttatus,* gets its name from the Greek *katharos,* "pure," referring to its song, and *gut-tata,* "spotted," for its typical thrush's spotted breast. It lives, hermitlike, in woody places where the wood thrush, also a fine songster, can be found, too. The hermit thrush was immortalized by Walt Whitman in "When Lilacs Last in the Dooryard Bloom'd." Apparently in 1865 John Burroughs described the hermit thrush to the poet and, said Burroughs, Whitman used "the information I have given him in one of his principal poems." The hermit thrush's "victorious song" more usually occurs at dawn or dusk than in the "black murk" of night, but surely, one feels, at least on this occasion there was an exception.

# TITMOUSE AND CHICKADEE

Tits and chickadees seem to like people and often "reply" to human whistles. The common name "titmouse" is from the Old Icelandic *titr,* meaning "small," and the Anglo-Saxon *mase,* "small bird." This is not the same root as "mouse" (from the Latin *mus*), and "titmice" as a plural is not etymologically consistent, even if these birds do seem a bit like perky little mice. The chickadee's name is onomatopoeic, from the sound of its call; the Cherokee Indians called it *tsikilili.*

Tits and chickadees perch upside down, searching for insects on branches, or feed aerobatically at bird tables, where they are frequent visitors. Their family name, Paridae, comes from the Roman name for tit, *parus.* Their common names (black, coal, blue, tufted, etc.) are generally descriptive of their appearance, but the mountain chickadee got its species name, *gambeli,* from Dr. William Gambel. Gambel discovered many new birds in the West (including a quail named for him), but died young of typhoid fever at a miners' camp in California. His last collection,

**The chickadee's name is onomatopoeic, from the sound of its call; the Cherokees called it *tsikilili*.** shipped home ahead of him, was lost when the vessel was wrecked. Tits are sometimes called tomtits, although their call is often described as sounding like "Peter, Peter, Peter."

Chickadees only molt once annually but their summer plumage protects them through the harshest winters, for they do not migrate to warmer climates. Emerson described his encounter with a tit on a freezing winter walk in his poem "The Titmouse." He found himself three miles from home and in danger of being "Embalmed by purifying cold." At just that moment a titmouse appeared:

> Here was this atom in full breath
> Hurling defiance at vast death.

In the poem the revived poet tells the bird he will remember "my debt," and in his notebook Emerson wrote, "I promised him crumbs, and must not go again to these woods without them." We do not know if the bird held him to his promise!

# Turkey

**W**hen the Spaniards came to the New World, the South Americans gave them turkeys, which the explorers had never seen before. The Indians had never seen horses before and, supposing them to be carnivorous animals, offered them turkeys too. In October 1511, Miguel de Passamonte, chief treasurer of the Indies, was ordered by the Spanish government to bring to Seville "well guarded, ten turkeys, half males and the other half females." Turkeys soon became common throughout Europe. But they were confused with guinea fowl, which have the same flecked plumage and had already been imported from Asia.

Guinea fowl were called "turkey hens" or *meleagris*. Meleager was a prince of Calydon, killed by a boar, whose sorrowing sisters were transformed into birds spattered or speckled (*meleagris* in Greek means "speckled") with tear stains. In the days when geography was a little vague, any rare bird imported from a far-away place, like Turkey, was called a turkey. And if from Turkey, why not from India? Both guinea fowl and turkeys were also called "cock from India" or *coq d'Inde,* shorted to *d'Indon. Dindon* is still French for "turkey." Now guinea fowls are in the family Numididae (from the country Numidia), and turkeys have taken the family name Meleagrididae.

*2.* **In the days when geography was a little vague, any rare bird imported from a faraway place, like Turkey, was called a turkey.**

North American settlers, not realizing that turkeys had originated in America, mistakenly thought that the wild turkeys they found were different from turkeys they had known in Europe. Some Native Americans used turkeys for food and feathers, but others eschewed them, be-lieving they might engender cowardice, since a turkey's response to an enemy is to run away. We are told that Indians gave the pilgrims turkey for their first Thanksgiving dinner, and by Alexander Hamilton's time he could say, "No cit-izen of the United States should refrain from turkey on Thanks-giving Day."

Ben Franklin proposed this "true original native of America" as our national bird, adding that it did not care for "red coats," the color of English military uniforms. The bare neck of a turkey cock is suffused with blood when it sees a rival, and the bird was believed to attack anything red. Actually, as its sexual enthusiasm is aroused, it "changeth from time to time, to al colours of the Rainebow . . . which colours ever altring, the byrd appearth as it were a myracle of nature," as a sixteenth-century book of husbandry put it.

Turkeys are expected to play an integral, and personally un-rewarding, role in many American celebrations. They may not have made it as our national bird, but surely they deserve to be recognized as honorable citizens.

# Vulture

The biblical vulture, from the mountains of Sinai, is the lammergeier (from the German *Lämmer,* "lamb," and *Geier,* "vulture"), because it was thought to take lambs. Actually the vulture eats offal and bones, extracting the nutritious marrow by dropping larger bones from on high down to a favorite stone or "ossuary." The Greek playwrite Aeschylus was said to have been killed by a vulture dropping a tortoise onto his bald head, mistakenly taking it to be a stone—presumably not a favorite one.

Legendary Old World vultures are widespread over Africa, Asia, and southern Europe but, although similar in habits and appearance, are not related to New World vultures, of the Cathartidae family (from the Greek *kathartes,* "a cleanser," because vultures clean up dead bodies.) The American turkey buzzard is a vulture, *Cathartes aura* ("aura" is probably a South American name for this bird). North American settlers, who gave them their common name, thought they looked a bit like turkeys and soared like European buzzards. Another vulture, the endangered California condor, is *Gymnogyps californianus* (from the Greek *gymnos,* "naked," for its bald head).

By convergent evolution, unrelated Old and New World vultures share some of the less charming avian characteristics. All vultures rely on others to kill their prey and many have bald heads and necks, which they can plunge into cadavers without soiling their feathers. They soar magnificently in continuous circles, looking for food. Because they are heavy, vultures can't easily take off, especially after a good meal. They have weak feet but strong beaks with which to tear at their food. Their shared common name comes from the Latin *vuellere,* "to tear."

The stomach acids of vultures are highly acidic and help dissolve the carrion they eat. The excreta of New World vultures is very acidic, too, and perhaps sterilizes their legs, over which they don't mind defecating. To discourage predators, or perhaps to become lighter and more agile, vultures have the inhospitable habit of vomiting up their last meal in the face of any creature that startles them.

The turkey buzzard has no voice box and makes only a hissing sound "exactly resembling that produced by thrusting a red hot poker into water," wrote Alexander Wilson. Its nostrils are perforated, allowing a clear view through its beak. It is now thought to detect its food by smell as well as sight, but the capacity of vultures to smell has caused much ornithological distress. John

Audubon and the British naturalist Charles Waterton had a vitriolic quarrel on the subject, complicated because they were probably talking about different kinds of vultures. It became absurd when a supporter of Audubon showed a painting of a sheep, skinned and cut open, to vultures. The birds tugged at the painting but were apparently disappointed and flew away.

**The Bible cautions that being eaten by vultures after death is the worst possible punishment for human misbehavior.**

The Bible repeatedly cautions that being eaten by vultures after death is the worst possible punishment for human misbehavior, because the Jews believed that a soul searched for rest eternally until the body was properly buried. But the Zoroastrian Parsis, who believed that earth, fire, and water were sacred to God and must not be polluted by death, built special open towers, where bodies were laid out to be eaten by vultures. Meanwhile the bereaved prayed in a garden nearby for the souls of the consumed dead to merge into the immortal sky.

# WAGTAIL

Wagtails wag their tails up and down. They move rapidly over the ground, searching for insects, and they often hunt near water. In French they were *battelessive* or *lavandière,* which, Pierre Belon wrote in 1555, was because they behaved like "a laundress beating her clothes." Long ago, when laundry was done in open streams, it was beaten with a special stick to loosen dirt, with an up-and-down motion similar to that of a wagtail's tail. The wagtails, wrote Belon, also "keep laundresses company along river banks." In Old English, wagtails were called washtail, or dishwasher, sometimes attached to a female name like Molly, or Polly, Dishwasher. So presumably they did the dishes as well as the laundry.

The wagtail's scientific name is a scholastic mistake, perpetuated over time. It is *Motacilla* and was traditionally thought to come from *mota,* "move," and *cilla,* "tail." But actually *cilla* isn't a word and doesn't mean "tail." Marcus Terentius Varro, the Roman scholar who named the bird, called it *motacilla,* or "little mover," the whole word being a diminutive from *movere* ("to move"). In his notes on the name he wrote that the bird "always moves its tail." Naturalists thought that *cilla* meant "tail" (even incorrectly naming waxwings Bomby*cilli*dae, "silken-tailed").

**2. The wagtail's scientific name is a scholastic mistake, perpetuated over time.**

The wagtail that is common in Ireland and Britain is called *M. alba yarrelli,* for William Yarrell. Yarrell wrote *History of British Birds* in 1837, the precise year that William MacGillivray published his book with exactly the same title. (Incidentally, Yarrell's book, which was half the length and better illustrated than MacGillivray's, sold much better—a lesson for authors?)

The wagtail family includes pipits and longclaws. The yellow wagtail, *M. flava* ("yellow"), nests in Alaska. Pipits (so called in imitation of their cry) are found worldwide. All wagtails have a long hind claw, but those of the longclaws are exceptionally long.

The European pied wagtail is *Motacilla alba,* from *alba,* "white." This wagtail is black and white, with a skull-like white face. Consequently, it was sometimes associated with death. But this bouncing, jolly bird really seems more at home in its role as a laundry maid, cheerfully chattering to its companions on the banks of bubbling streams.

# WARBLER

It is tempting to suspect that warblers were created in order to provide worthy employment for ornithologists. There are two kinds of warblers, the Old World warblers and the New World warblers, and they are not related. At this time, the Old World warblers are in the Sylviidae family, and the New World warblers seem to be in the Parulinae subfamily of the Ember- izidae (bunting) family. It seems superfluous to add that if they have been moved it will not be for the first time! Meanwhile, the name of the Old World, or Sylviidae, warblers comes from the Latin *sylva*, meaning "wood," but it is the parulid (New World) warblers that are commonly called wood-warblers. When it comes to warbler names, most of us are lost in the woods.

The warbler's common name comes from *werble,* which first meant a tune and then meant to sing sweetly. The root, *wirbil* in Old German, meant a "whirlwind," or the act of twirling oneself around (and singing?). Anyway, neither Old nor New World warblers necessarily "warble," their songs and habits varying as much as they do. The *Locustella,* or grasshopper warblers, sound a bit like insects (locusts) or the reeling in of a fishing line.

**New World warblers arrive in great numbers, which ornithologists call "warbler waves."**

Old World warblers are spread over Europe, Africa, Asia, and Australia. Because they search through foliage for insects, many Old World warblers are named *Phylloscopus* (from the Greek *phullus,* "a leaf," and *skopos,* "a watchman"). The European chiffchaff (so called for its two-note song) is *P. collybita,* meaning "a moneylender," apparently because its song sounds like jingling coins. A large group of Old World warblers is the *Acrocephalus* ("sharp-headed"), a name that reflects the narrow heads and sharp-pointed bills of warblers. Many New World warblers are in the *Dendroica* genus, from the Greek *dendron,* meaning "a tree," which is where they like to live. *Vermivora* like to eat "worms."

Warblers often build beautiful nests, and the Old World warblers include the tailorbirds, which pierce the edges of leaves, using fibers or cobwebs to stitch them together into cones. American ovenbirds are warblers that make dome-shaped nests, like old ovens. But the prothonotary warbler (also from the New World) nests in holes. Its common name comes from its yellow plumage, the color of robes worn by papal clerks, or prothonotaries, when they met to confirm beatifications, canonizations, or other weighty matters.

Most New World warblers live in the tropics, but many come to nest in North America. They arrive in great numbers, which ornithologists call "warbler waves." Many of them look quite different in fall. The nuptial plumage of returning adults has faded, and the young birds haven't yet got adult markings, so it is harder than ever to identify them. Roger Tory Peterson's popular bird guide has a whole section entitled "Confusing Fall Warblers." Apparently the Cherokee Indians, who named many birds, didn't even try to sort warblers (and they only had parulids to contend with!). That doesn't seem to stop some of us from trying. Peterson himself once said, "If it were not for the warblers, birding would lose half its fun." As for the rest of us, ornithologists might not approve, but (at least in autumn) we could always presume that the bird we can't identify is "a warbler."

# WOODCOCK AND SNIPE

Woodcocks and snipe share the dubious privilege of being the only legal game birds in the sandpiper family. A seventeenth-century medical book warned that as a table bird the "snite" was even "worse than the Woodcocke, being more un-pleasant to the taste . . . and very apt to engender melancholy." Unfortunately for both birds this perception has not generally been shared by lovers of game.

As well as being good to eat, woodcocks and snipe share other characteristics: both can be found worldwide; both use their feathers as sounding instruments in their courtship flight; and both use their long thin bills (which have movable tips) to probe for food.

Woodcocks are chubbier than snipe, with rounded wings and shorter legs, and (logically) they live in the woods. Their Anglo-Saxon name was *wudu-cocc* or *wude snite*. They lie low during the day, mostly feeding at night and mostly eating worms. Some-times they stamp first to disturb the worms, which when caught are sucked up whole. Woodcocks have very large protruding eyes that allow the birds to see above and behind. Their brain is tilted so far back it is almost upside down, conveniently counteracting the bird's usual position with its head down and its bill stuck into the ground. Woodcocks were once named *Philohela,* meaning "bog loving," but now they are *Scolopax* (Greek for a woodcock). The American woodcock is *Scolopax minor,* because it is smaller than its Eurasian counterpart, *S. rusticola* ("rustic"). Because they lie low in woods, hunters would flush out "woodcocks" with specially trained dogs, called "cocker" spaniels.

**Because they lie low in woods, hunters would flush out woodcocks with specially trained dogs, called "cocker" spaniels.**

Snipe and woodcocks were caught with nets until guns accurate enough to shoot them were developed. When startled, snipe rise suddenly with a characteristic zigzag flight, and shooting one is a challenge to hunters. A good marksman is consequently called a "sniper." A group of flying snipe is called a "wisp," most likely because it looks like a trail of smoke.

The common snipe is widespread in Europe and America. It is now *Gallinago gallinago,* from the Latin *gallo,* meaning "a hen," which is about the same size. Its former name, however, was *Capella gallinago,* using the feminine of the Latin *caper,* "a goat." In Scotland snipe were called "heather bleaters," and a Cornish name for them was "gaverhal," from the Cornish *gavar,* "a goat." These names clearly derived from the sound snipe make during their mating rituals, when special outer tail feathers, stiffened with extra barbules, vibrate to make a curious bleating sound as air passes through them.

The woodcock also uses its feathers to make nuptial sounds, not with its tail but with three stiff outer feathers on its wings. Eurasian male woodcocks look for females by "roding" (from the Anglo-Saxon "raid"). The male bird flies purposefully in circles until he successfully locates a receptive female. When he has found a mate, he doesn't let her out of his sight until she has laid the eggs, which he then can be sure are his own. Afterward he resumes his display flights to attract another female, while the first incubates the eggs!

# WOODPECKER

Picus, the king of Latium, unwisely repulsed Circe's advances, so she changed him into a woodpecker. Circe was a specialist in metamorphosis, best known for turning Odysseus's men into swine. Picus, although a god and the son of Saturn, was clearly no match for her, and she easily "chang'd his form who could not change his heart," wrote Dryden. Picus gave his name to the Picidae, or woodpecker family.

Woodpeckers get much of their food by drilling into wood for insects and grubs, extracting them with incredibly long tongues (*see* Flicker). They excavate nesting cavities, which other less well equipped birds later take over. Their bills and skulls have evolved uniquely to enable them to pound wood hard and rapidly, in some species at speeds up to twenty blows a second. The brains of few creatures could survive such a battering without damage. They don't have much cerebrospinal fluid, so woodpeckers' brains are packed tightly into the skull and can't "bounce" against it, causing harm. Woodpeckers have a muscular pad at the back of their lower jaw that also acts as a shock absorber. The bill itself is very dense and has a chisel-like, self-sharpening edge. By contrast, the toucan, also a piciforme, has a seemingly massive bill that is actually light and fragile. Because the toucan eats fruit, its bill developed more for show than power.

> **The brain is packed tightly into the skull and can't "bounce" against it, causing harm.**

A woodpecker walks up trees using its stiff tail as a prop. The pointed tail feathers stick into bark crevices for extra support. Unlike most birds, the tail feathers molt from outward to inward, so the supporting central feathers are retained longest.

A common American woodpecker is the little downy woodpecker, *Picoides pubescens*. Linnaeus, who was no prude about sex, named it *pubescens* because its downy plumage was, he thought, like nascent genital hair at puberty. Linnaeus called the ivory-billed woodpecker *Picus principalis,* meaning "princely," a sad concept now that this magnificent bird is probably extinct. Its scientific name is now *Campephilus principalis,* "princely grub lover." Alexander Wilson caught an ivory-billed woodpecker and marveled at its "unconquerable spirit." He described its cry as "exactly resembling the violent crying of a young child," as his captive tried to escape before it died.

The woodpecker was often compared to a lonely woodsman clearing trees, and they are solitary birds. Another name for them was a hewel, or hew-hole. "No doubt the incessant hewing of holes, without adequate object, would be sufficiently miserable," wrote Wilson, but "these, however, are the pleasures of the bird."

Woodpeckers flourish in thick forests with decaying trees, habitats that humans tend to destroy. In many cultures they are considered gods with special powers. They were often thought able to bring rain and in France were called *pics de la pluie*. Maybe, in spite of Circe's spell, the woodpecker did retain some of its godlike power. But if we continue to destroy its forests it will have no place to live—and even gods need to live somewhere.

# WREN

He who shall hurt the little wren,
Shall never be beloved by men.

So wrote William Blake, and wrens in Britain were protected except on Saint Stephen's Day, when there was a
"wren hunt." A captured wren was taken from house to
house and then killed and buried with whimsical solemnity. The
magical associations of this ritual are obscure, but the wren was
believed to have special powers.

The ancients called the tiny European wren, which darts from
bush to bush wagging its perpendicular tail, *trockhilos*. This was

the name of a small clever bird said to dive into the mouths of crocodiles to clean their teeth (*see* Hummingbird). The wren was sometimes called the "king of the birds" for supposedly out-witting the eagle in a contest to fly highest. It did this by perching on the eagle's back to gain height!

All wrens are thought to have originated in North America and then spread to South America, where most of the family is found. However, one kind of wren is believed, sometime in pre-history, to have crossed the Bering Strait and spread over Asia and Europe and still nests in Alaska too. In America this wren is called the winter wren, and in Europe it is the only wren. Its name is *Troglodytes troglodytes,* meaning "cave dweller," from the Greek *trogle,* "hole," and *dytes,* "a burrower." Wrens dive into their nest holes, once in hollow trees but now in anything hollow they find, including the pockets of coats left hanging in a tool shed.

The American house wren, *T. aedon,* gets its name because of a mythological error. Aëdon was an unpleasingly jealous Theban queen. Her sister-in-law Niobe had six sons and Aëdon had only one, Itylus. She resolved to equal the balance somewhat by elim-inating one of her nephews, but Itylus was asleep in the same room as his cousins, and she mistook his bed for her nephew's. When she discovered that she had killed her own son (some ac-counts have him cooked and served up to his father), she asked to be changed into a bird and became a nightingale (*not* a wren!). In some versions all the members of the family were turned into different birds — an avian insult not unique to this classical fable.

The wren, often affectionately called jenny wren, was believed to be the demure wife of robin redbreast. The wren's behavior, as we now know, can be anything but demure. In 1925 jenny wren lost some of her credentials when Miss Althea Sherman, in the March issue of the *Wilson Bulletin,* wrote "Case of the People of America Versus the House Wren," demanding that "the felon be sentenced" for attacking other birds, usurping their nests, and even killing their young.

**♫ Wrens nest in holes, including the pockets of coats.**

Possibly, the origin of the name "wren" is from the Anglo-Saxon *wroene,* "lascivious," or else from the Swedish *vrensk,* "uncastrated." At one time prostitutes were called "wrens." Female members of the British navy are also called Wrens, from WRNS (Women's Royal Naval Service), *not* because they look or behave like the bird of that name.

# SELECTED BIBLIOGRAPHY

Alexander, W. B. *Birds of the Ocean* (G.P. Putnam's Sons, 1954).

Allen, Glover Morrill. *Birds and their Attitudes* (Marsh Jones, 1925).

Allen, Robert Porter. *The Flamingos: Their Life, History, and Survival* (National Audubon Society, 1956).

Armstrong, Edward A. *A Study of Bird Song* (Dover, 1973).

———. *The Folklore of Birds* (Houghton Mifflin, 1959).

———. *The Life and Lore of the Bird* (Crown, 1959).

Attenborough, David. *The Life of Birds* (Princeton University Press, 1998).

Baker, Kevin. *Warblers of Europe, Asia, and North Africa* (Princeton University Press, 1997).

Batty, J. *Domesticated Ducks & Geese* (Spur Publications, 1979).

Bent, Arthur Cleveland. *Life Histories of North American Birds* (20 volumes, republished Dover, 1960's).

Berger, Andrew J. *Bird Study* (Dover, 1961).

Bildstein, Keith C. *White Ibis* (Smithsonian Institute, 1993).

Bird, David. *The Bird Almanac* (Firefly Books, 1999).

Blanchan, Neltje. *Bird Neighbors* (Doubleday, 1904).

Blessingame, Wyatt. *Wonders of Egrets Bitterns & Herons* (Dodd Mead, 1983).

Boswall, Jeffery. *Birds for all Seasons* (BBC Publications, 1986).

Brewer, T. M. *Wilson's American Ornithology* (H.S. Samuels, 1839).

Brosse, Jacques. *Great Voyages of Discovery* (Facts on File, 1983).

Burroughs, John. *Wake-Robin* (Houghton Mifflin, 1897).

Burton, Robert. *Bird Behaviour* (Alfred A. Knopf, 1985).

Butten, D., and D. Hayashida. *The Japanese Crane* (Kodansha, 1981).

Byers, C., J. Curson, and U. Olsson. *Sparrows and Buntings* (Houghton Mifflin, 1995).

Campbell, Bruce, and Elizabeth Lack. *A Dictionary of Birds* (Buteo Books, 1985).

Choate, Earnest A. *Dictionary of American Bird Names* (Harvard, 1985).

Claiborne, Robert. *Loose Cannons & Red Herrings* (W.W. Norton, 1988).

Cleere, Nigel. *Nightjars* (Yale University, 1998).

Cokinos, Christopher. *Hope Is the Thing with Feathers* (Tarcher/Putnam, 2000).

Cruickshank, Allen and Helen Cruickshank. *1001 Questions Answered about Birds* (Dover, 1958).

Cruickshank, Helen. *Thoreau on Birds* (McGraw Hill, 1964).

Delacour, Jean. *Pheasants of the World* (Spur Publications, 1977).

Dorst, Jean. *The Life of Birds* (Columbia University, 1974).

Doughty, Robin. *Feather Fashions & Bird Preservation* (University of California Press, 1975).

Druce, D.C. *The Caladrius & Its Legend* (Archaeological Journal, 1912).

Eifert, Virginia. *Men, Birds & Adventure* (Dodd, Mead & Co., 1962).

Egremont, Pamela. *The Calculating Cormorants* (Linnaean Society, 1979).

Elrod, C., and H. Wilborn. *The Ratite Encyclopedia* (Ratite Records, 1995).

Feare, C., and A. Craig. *Starlings & Mynahs* (Princeton University Press, 1999).

Feduccia, Alan, ed. *Catesby's Birds of Colonial America* (University of North Carolina Press, 1985).

Fisher, James. *The Shell Bird Book* (Ebury Press & Michael Joseph, 1966).

Ford, Alice. *Audubon by Himself* (Natural History Press, 1967).

Forsyth, Adrian. *The Nature of Birds* (Camden House, 1988).

Freeman, Margaret. *The Unicorn Tapestries* (Metropolitan Museum, 1983).

Friedmann, Herbert. *The Symbolic Goldfinch* (Pantheon, 1946).

Firth, C., and B. Beehler. *The Birds of Paradise* (Oxford University, 1998).

Gingras, Pierre. *The Secret Lives of Birds* (Firefly Books, 1995).

Glardon, Philippe. (facsimile of 1555 edition) *Pierre Belon du Mans L'Histoire de la Nature des Oyseaux* (Libraire Droz, 1997).

Gooders, J., and T. Boyer. *Ducks of North America* (Facts on File, 1986).

Gorman, James. *The Total Penguin* (Prentice Hall, 1990).

Gotch, A. F. *Latin Names Explained* (Facts on File, 1995).

Graham, Frank. *Gulls, A Social History* (Random House, 1975).

Grosvenor, Gilbert, ed. *The Book of Birds* (National Geographic Society, 1937).

Gruson, Edward. *Words for Birds* (Quadrangle Books, 1972).

Harting, James. *The Birds of Shakespeare* (Argonaut, 1965).

Harrison, Peter. *Seabirds of the World* (Princeton University Press, 1996).

Hartley, G. Innes. *The Importance of Bird Life* (Century, 1922).

Hays, H. R. *Birds, Beasts & Men* (G.P. Putnam's Sons, 1972).

Heinrich, Bernd. *Ravens in Winter* (Barrie & Jenkins, 1990).

————. *The Mind of the Raven* (Cliff Street Books, 1999).

Hendrickson, John. *Birds of Prey* (Chronicle Books, 1992).

Heron-Allen, E. *Barnacles in Nature & Myth* (Oxford University Press, 1928).

Hill, Jen. *An Exhilaration of Wings* (Viking, 1999).

Houston, David. *Birds of Prey* (Facts on File, 1990).

Hume, Rob. *Owls of the World* (Running Press, 1991).

Hunter, Clark. *The Life & Letters of Alexander Wilson* (American Philosophical Society, 1983).

Ingersoll, Ernest. *Birds in Legend Fable & Folklore* (Longmans, Green, 1923).

Irmscher, Christopher, ed. *John James Audubon* (Library of America, 1999).

Jackson, C. *Great Bird Paintings of the World* (Antique Collectors Club, 1993).

James, Ivor. *The Source of the Ancient Mariner* (Folcroft Press, 1969).

Jobling, James. *A Dictionary of Scientific Bird Names* (Oxford University Press, 1995).

Johns, C. A. *British Birds in their Haunts* (reprint, Routledge & Kegan, 1948).

Johnsgard, Paul. *Crane Music* (Smithsonian Institute, 1991).

—————. *Game and Quail in North America* (University of Nebraska Press, 1973).

—————. *Waterfowl* (University of Nebraska Press, 1968).

Jonsson, Lars. *Birds of Europe, North Africa & the Middle East* (Princeton University Press, 1995).

Kalm, Peter. *Travels in North America* (Dover, 1964).

Kastner, Joseph. *A World of Watchers* (Alfred A. Knopf, 1968).

Kligerman, Jack. *A Fancy for Pigeons* (Hawthorn, 1978).

Krutch, Joseph Wood. *A Treasury of Bird Lore* (Doubleday, 1962).

Lack, David. *The Life of the Robin* (Fontana, 1972).

Lambourne, Maureen. *The Art of Bird Illustration* (Grange Books, 1997).

Lawrence, R. D. *Owls, The Silent Fliers* (Firefly Books, 1997).

Leahy, Christopher. *The Birdwatcher's Companion* (Gramercy Books, 1982).

Lefranc, Norbert. *Shrikes* (Yale University, 1997).

Lockwood, W. B. *The Oxford Book of British Bird Names* (Oxford University Press, 1984).

Löfgren, Lars. *Ocean Birds* (Crescent Books, 1984).

Long, Kim. *Owls* (Johnson Books, 1998).

Lutwack, Leonard. *Birds in Literature* (University of Florida Press, 1994).

Masko, Jonathan. *The Owl Papers* (Dutton, 1982).

Marsh, George Perkins. *Man and Nature* (Scribner, 1864).

Massingham, H. J., ed. *Poems about Birds* (Fisher Unwin, 1922).

Mathews, Schuyler. *Field Book of Wild Birds & their Music* (Putnam's, 1904).

Matthiesson, Peter. *The Wind Birds* (Chapters Pub., 1994).

Martin, Laura. *The Folklore of Birds* (Globe/Pequot Press, 1993).

McClatchy, J. D. *On Wings of Song* (Alfred A. Knopf, 2000).

McIntyre, Judith. *The Common Loon* (University of Minnesota Press, 1986).

Mearns, B. and R. *Audubon to Xantus, the Lives of those Commemorated in North American Bird Names* (Academic Press, 1992).

Meinzer, Wyman. *The Roadrunner* (Texas Tech University Press, 1993).

Meyerriecks, Andrew. *Man & Birds* (Pegasus, 1972).

Middleton, Alex. *The American Goldfinch* (Stackpole Books, 1998).

Moses, Barry. *Word Mysteries & Histories* (Houghton Mifflin, 1986).

Netherton, John. *At the Water's Edge* (Voyeur Press, 1994).

Newton, Alfred. *A Dictionary of Birds* (Adam & Charles Black, 1893).

Nixton, Bob. *Dreambirds* (Picador, 1999).

Ovians, Gordon. *Blackbirds of America* (University of Washington Press, 1985).

Parmelee, Alice. *All the Birds of the Bible* (Harper & Brothers, 1959).

Pearson, Gilbert. *Birds of America* (Garden City Books, 1936).

Peterson, Roger Tory. *Birds Over America* (Grosset & Dunlap, 1948).

Poolman, Kenneth. *The Speedwell Voyage* (Berkley Books, 2000).

Price, Jennifer. *Flight Maps* (Basic Books, 1999).

Reilly, Pauline. *Penguins of the World* (Oxford University Press, 1994).

Richardson, Gary. *The Downy Woodpecker* (Stackpole Books, 1999).

Rising, James. *A Guide to the Identification & Natural History of the Sparrows of the United States & Canada* (Academic Press, 1996).

Robertson, Peter. *Pheasants* (Voyageur Press, 1997).

Root, Waverley. *Food* (Simon & Schuster, 1980).

Rothschild, M., and T. Clay. *Fleas, Flukes & Cuckoos* (Philosophical Library, 1952).

Salvin, Osbert, ed. *Barton's Fragments* (Philadelphia, 1799).

Saunders, Arelas. *A Guide to Bird Songs* (Doubleday, 1951).

Savage, Candace. *Bird Brains* (Sierra Club, 1995).

———. *Peregrine Falcons* (Sierra Club, 1992).

Schorger, A. W. *The Passenger Pigeon* (University of Wisconsin, 1955).

———. *The Wild Turkey* (University of Oklahoma, 1966).

Sherman, Paul. *Birds of a feather lek together* (Nature, Sept. 1999).

Shipman, Pat. *Taking Wing* (Simon & Schuster, 1998).

Sibley, David. *The Sibley Guide to Birds* (Alfred A. Knopf, 2000).

Simon, André. *A Concise Encyclopedia of Gastronomy* (Overlook Press, 1981).

Singer, Arthur and Alan. *State Birds* (Lodestar Books, 1986).

Simpson, George G. *Penguins Past and Present* (Yale University Press, 1976).

Skeat, Walter. *Etymological Dictionary* (Oxford University Press, 1879, reprint, 1997).

Smith, Susan. *Black-capped Chickadee* (Cornell University Press, 1991).

Skutch, Alexander. *Birds Asleep* (University of Texas Press, 1989).

————. *The Minds of Birds* (Texas A&M University Press, 1996).

————. *Life of the Hummingbird* (Crown, 1973).

————. *Life of the Flycatcher* (University of Oklahoma Press, 1997).

————. *Life of the Pigeon* (Cornell University Press, 1991).

————. *Parent Birds & their Young* (Texas University Press, 1979).

Snyder, N. and H. *Study of Mollusc Predation* (Ornithology Lab., Cornell, 1969).

Soǔrex, Otakur. *Antonin Dvořák,* trans. P. Samson (De Capo Press, 1958).

Sparks, J., and T. Soper. *Parrots, A Natural History* (Facts on File, 1978).

————. *Penguins* (Facts on File, 1987).

Spencer, Colin. *The Heretic's Feast* (University of New England, 1995).

Staeble, A. E. *Number of Feathers in the English Sparrow* (Wilson Bull, 1943).

Stillson, Blanche. *Wings* (Bobbs-Merrill, 1954).

Stokes, Ted. *Birds of the Atlantic Ocean* (Country Life Books, 1968).

Streseman, Erwin. *Baron von Pernau* (The Auk, 1947).

————. *Ornithology from Aristotle to the Present* (Harvard University Press, 1975).

Summers, Denis. *The Sparrows. A study of the Genus Passer* (Doyser, 1988).

Swann, Kirke. *Dictionary of English & Folk-Names of British Birds* (Witherby, 1913).

Thompson, A. Landsborough. *A New Dictionary of Birds* (McGraw-Hill, 1964).

Thompson, Keith. *Man and the Natural World* (Pantheon, 1981).

Tinbergen, Niko. *Curious Naturalists* (American Museum of Natural History, 1969).

Wade, Nicholas, ed. *Science Times Book of Birds* (Lyons Press, 1997).

Wauer, Roland. *The American Robin* (University of Texas Press, 1999).

Weed, C., and N. Dearborn. *Birds in their Relations to Man* (Lippincott, 1924).

Weimerskirch and Wilson. *Oceanic Respite for Wandering Albatrosses* (Nature, 2000).

Welker, Robert. *Birds & Men* (Harvard University Press, 1955).

Welty, Joel. *The Life of Birds* (W. B. Saunders, 1962).

Wetmore, Alexander. *Birds of North America* (National Geographic, 1962).

White, Gilbert. *Natural History & Antiquities of Selbourne* (Macmillan, 1911).

White, T. H. *The Bestiary*. Translation Twelfth-century Latin. (Capricorn, 1960).

Xenophon, Theodor. *Human Nature of Birds* (St. Martin's Press, 1993).

Yoon, C. K. "Hummingbirds Bear Mixed Gift to Flowers," *The New York Times,* (May 1995).

# INDEX